Knit

Alice Hoyle

Dynamic patterns
and techniques for
creative making

Knit

Alice Hoyle

Dynamic patterns
and techniques for
creative making

K

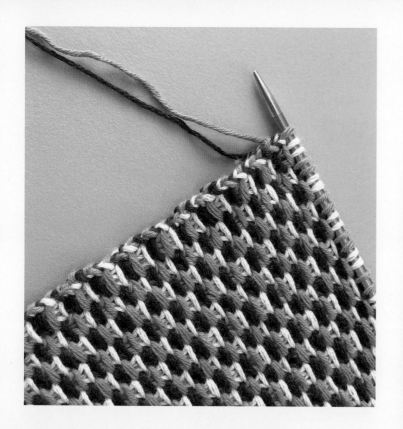

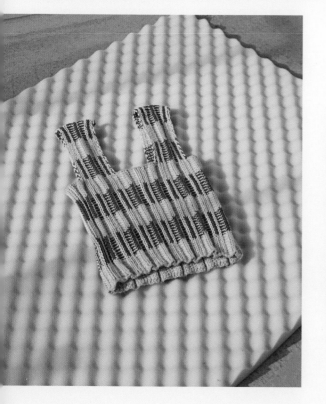

Contents

Introduction

There is something incredibly exciting and freeing in the ability to create anything with just your hands, needles, and yarn. The gradual, cathartic process of each stitch and row builds up to form a one-of-a-kind piece, with its own unique story to tell.

For me, the magic of this craft lies in researching and learning new techniques. Exploring stitches online and in sourcebooks reveals a world of possibilities and combinations, in the way stitches can be manipulated to create incredible textures.

Through my knitwear platform ROWS, my goal is to connect people with the vast potential of knitting, encouraging others to try different stitches and experience the same sense of amazement that I do when discovering the creative possibilities within this craft.

My Mum and Grandma introduced me to the basics of knitting as a child, and while my Grandma was an exceptional knitter, I only managed to create some holey and wavy-edged scarves. It wasn't until I started my art foundation course at college that I found knit was a medium I could use to express my creativity and ideas.

I studied fashion knitwear design at university, focusing predominantly on machine-based knitting, where I found myself more drawn to shape and sculpture in garments, than to stitch and texture. As part of the course I spent a year working in Hong Kong, an invaluable experience that sparked an excitement for color, which remains an integral part of my work today. After graduating I moved to London to work for Wool and the Gang, where I fell back in love with hand knitting and developed my pattern-writing skills.

When I relocated to Amsterdam, I took the opportunity to work on my own designs, experimenting with stitch as well as unraveling and cutting up old jumpers and scarves to use as yarn. I could write knitting patterns at this point, but had limited knowledge of traditional hand-knitting conventions. I was curiously exploring the possibilities of knitting.

I discovered the potential of using simple slip stitches to form vertical lines of color, something I thought was limited to more complex colorwork methods. From that moment on, my work became increasingly stitch based—the structure of a stitch and the way it was knitted formed the basis of an idea. I started to develop my first few patterns and the world I wanted them to live in: ROWS.

In my work, I find inspiration in patterns, textures, and the interaction of color in everyday life, as well as from second-hand, vintage, art, and woven textiles. I then translate these sources through stitches, color, yarn, and shape. I am continually inspired by seeing others bring my designs to life and this has proven to be the most rewarding aspect of what I do through ROWS. The incredible knitting community has shown me this craft is a powerful, vibrant, evolving art form.

Knit is a celebration of some of my favorite stitches, found and developed throughout my journey with ROWS so far. Within this book, you'll find a diverse collection of 16 knitting patterns, ranging from accessories and garments to homeware as well as ideas I have explored around yarn, considering ways to use up leftovers and how to repurpose unwanted materials. The stitches featured in this book are often easier to knit than they look, so give it a go, experiment with yarns and color, and keep exploring the joy of this amazing craft.

All about yarn

Knit

Choosing yarn

We encourage you to explore any fibers and colors that you love. Whether you opt for new yarn, second-hand finds or utilize what you already have, our collection of stitches and patterns can be a canvas for your own ideas.

To help you choose your yarn, the patterns in this book use standard weights. The table below outlines the yarn weight terminology we use, along with the average stockinette stitch gauge for each category:

Yarn weight	Stitches per 4"
Lace	33–40 sts
Fingering	27–32 sts
Sport	23–26 sts
DK	21–24 sts
Worsted	16–20 sts
Bulky	12–15 sts
Super Bulky	7–11 sts

Each pattern includes all the information for the yarns that we have used, along with recommended substitutions. If you want a similar outcome to our pieces, you can refer to these as a guide when selecting your yarn. To check if a yarn is suitable for the pattern, you can compare the standard stockinette stitch gauge indicated on the ball band with the suggested yarn. When using yarn that doesn't have a ball band, it's helpful to compare the thickness to other yarns that you already have and are familiar with in terms of weight.

We're continually searching for ways to utilize the yarns and materials we already have. In the following pages, we will explore some creative ideas for using leftover yarn and look at alternative methods for generating yarn.

Working with your yarn stash

The challenge of using up half-balls and odd balls of yarn left over from past projects can often lead to creative processes and outcomes. Here are a few suggestions on how you can adapt the patterns in this book to make use of yarns that you already have.

Projects featuring stockinette and garter stitch provide the ideal base for stripes using leftover half-balls of yarn. We have used cotton DK leftovers to create this playful take on the original Sol top (page 120).[Photo 1] This would work equally well for The wrap around (page 70) and the Mix up blanket (page 88).

Leftover yarn also works well in stitch patterns. In the Ziggy sweater (page 94), for example, four mixed-weight yarns are striped, working four rows in each color throughout.[Photo 2] This makes it ideal to swap for leftover yarn—ignore the color references and instead work four rows in each of your leftover yarns.

Photo 1

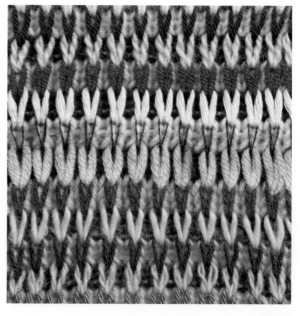

Photo 2

In vertical stripe patterns such as the Escher beanie (page 48), intersecting stripes in leftover yarns can create a color change effect where three colors meet at once.[Photo 3] Only two colors are used for each stripe, but they change color at different intervals, resulting in overlapping colors instead of distinct stripes.

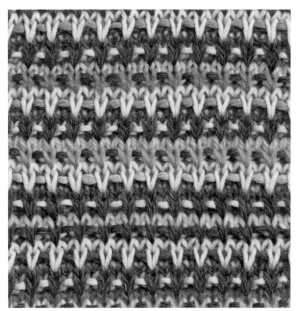

Photo 4

Photo 3

Here's what we did: After working 3 rounds in color B, change to a new color B yarn. From this point onwards change the color B yarn after every 6 rounds worked in color B. Change the color A yarn after working 6 rounds in color A, throughout.

Replacing one color with leftover yarns works well for the Echo scarf (page 112): If you keep color A (gray) and color B (white) but replace color C with leftover yarn, the stitch transforms to create a mock Fair Isle pattern.[Photo 4] This could also work well for any two-color patterns, such as the Wave vest (page 64) and the Rush hood (page 84).

Holding multiple yarns together is an easy way to use up leftover yarn. In this example of the Drift jacket (page 128), we used a light blue worsted-weight yarn throughout but mixed it with two strands of DK-weight leftover yarns, swapping each out as needed.[Photo 5]

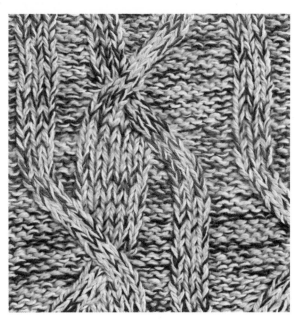

Photo 5

Working with yarn scraps

After collecting our leftover scraps of yarn, like a lot of knitters, we've been looking for various ways to use them. Here are just a few ideas:

- Knot all the ends together to make a multi-color scrap yarn ball to knit into a new project.
- Add personalized embroidery to a project, a beautiful way to incorporate scraps.
- Create tassels for scarves or pompoms for hats.
- Use for stuffing in projects that require it.
- Explore thrumming projects, a technique we share below.
- If you're interested in spinning, create recycled yarn (this is the dream!). Brush the scraps into fibers and spin them into unique artisanal yarns.

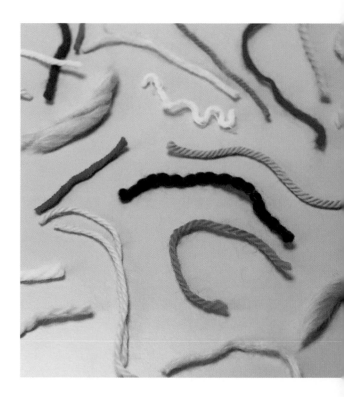

Thrumming

This technique involves pulling small pieces of yarn through knitted fabric to create a layer of tassels on one side and duplicate stitches on the others side. Originally, the term 'thrum' referred to the leftover pieces of thread that held no value after a fabric was woven. Traditionally, this technique uses wool roving to create a warm lining for mittens, but we think it's the perfect way to use up small scraps of yarn. We have used this technique on a stockinette stitch base for the Scrappy cushion (page 116).

RS duplicate stitch

WS tassels

How to thrum 1 stitch:

1. Insert your right needle through the stitch below the first stitch on the left needle.[Photo 1]

Photo 1   Photo 2

2. Take a small piece of yarn approx. 5½in long— this is your thrum. The length of the thrum may vary with your scraps (we have worked with pieces as small as 3in); you may also wish to double up if you are using a finer piece of yarn. Fold it in half and wrap the centre around the right needle.[Photo 2]

3. Draw the piece of yarn through the stitch.[Photo 3]

Photo 3   Photo 4

4. Insert the right needle through the first stitch on the left needle and complete a normal knit stitch.[Photos 4 & 5]

5. Slip the piece of yarn over the knit stitch.[Photos 6 & 7]

Photo 5   Photo 6

6. Pull down on the piece of yarn at the back to neaten the thrum.[Photo 8]

Photo 7   Photo 8

Reusing yarn

Unraveling something you no longer wear is a great way to generate yarn for a new project. You can unravel something you've knitted yourself by unpicking all the seams, undoing the Bind off edges, and unraveling from there. You can unravel a shop-bought garment by using the steps below. While it's not a quick process, it's interesting to watch the transformation and gain insights into garment manufacturing along the way.

Useful tools: Stitch unpicker (or small scissors if you don't have one), sharp fabric scissors, and something to wind the yarn around, such as a large book or yarn swift.

Before starting the process, it's essential to check a few things to ensure you can successfully unravel. If the garment has been cut and sewn together it won't unravel continuously, so we recommend picking a sweater, as cardigan plackets are often cut and sewn.

Check the seams inside the garment and look for seams joined using the linking method (see photo, above left). This indicates that the panels were knitted to size and not cut. When you turn the seam to one side, you should see a chain stitch up the seam that can be easily unpicked (see photo, above right). Differentiate between the thread used for the chain stitch and the yarn itself, as you only want to unpick the thread.

Linked seam   Linked seam side view

Unpicking and Unraveling

1. Turn the sweater inside out and use a stitch unpicker to remove all the care and brand labels.[Photo 1]

2. To unpick all the seams, start on one side of the garment. Typically the sleeve underarm seam and the body side seam are one long seam. Look for the chain stitch on the seam and start at the end where the chain stitch sits in the direction shown above. Use a stitch unpicker to start unpicking the stitch and you should find that you can pull on the thread and ease the seam open.[Photos 2 & 3] Repeat for the other sleeve underarm seam and body side seam.

3. In the same way, unpick the armhole seams, separating the sleeves from the body. Next, unpick the neckline, and finally, the shoulder seams.[Photos 4 & 5] You should now have flat panels ready to be unraveled.[Photo 6]

4. Unravel each panel from the top to the bottom. You may need to prepare the top of each panel. Sometimes, another line of stitching needs to be unpicked to reveal live stitches. Sometimes, the top of the front and back panels can be messy after unpicking the neck trim. You may need to cut a straight line[Photo 7] below any shaping, so that you can start to unravel the panel from this point. The first few rows may be untidy but then it will start to unravel easily. Keep all the scraps to use for later projects and sewing seams.

5. Unravel each panel, winding the yarn around something like a book[Photo 8] to create a hank, or directly to a yarn swift if you have one. Before removing, tie small pieces of thread or yarn tightly in several places.[Photo 9]

6. Wash the hanks the same way you would block something, then hang them up to dry.

7. Once fully dry, wind each hank into a ball of yarn.[Photo 10] On page 70, you can see what we knitted. If you're unsure about the yarn weight, compare it to other yarns you already have.

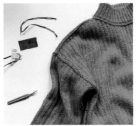

Photo 1

Photo 2

Photo 3

Photo 4

Photo 5

Photo 6

Photo 7

Photo 8

Photo 9

Photo 10

Turning fabric into yarn

Repurposing unwanted fabric is a fun way to create textural yarn for knitting into more structured pieces such as the Helix bag (page 124). All you need is your unwanted fabrics, a sharp pair of fabric scissors, and a tape measure.

As with any project, it's good to consider which fabrics you want to work with based on the end use. Lightweight yet durable fabrics, such as a light cotton, work well for the Helix bag. If you are looking to make something heavier and more textural, you could try denim, whereas for something more delicate, you could try working with silk.

This technique can be applied to fabrics of all sizes. Working with a larger piece of fabric, such as a bedsheet, means you can create a large amount of continuous yarn to use for a project. On the other hand, working with smaller pieces of fabric, such as a top or pillowcase, enables you to incorporate several fabrics together into one project.

Preparing the fabric

Cut your fabric into a clean rectangle, removing any seams, edging, or components. For example, if you are using a sheet, cut around the edges to remove any stitching or elastic.

Cutting smaller fabrics into yarn

This is the basic principle for cutting fabric into a continuous strip of yarn.[fig. 1] Using fabric scissors, cut where the dotted lines are—the arrows show where to start that line of cutting.

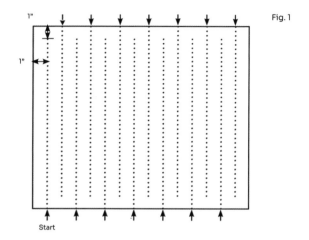

Fig. 1

1. Start at the first arrow labelled 'start'. Measure 1in from the edge and start cutting in a straight line (this is our chosen yarn width for the Helix bag, but depending on your fabric you may want to experiment with this). Stop approx. 1in before the end of the fabric.

2. For the next cut, go to the other side of the fabric where the opposite arrow is, measure 1in from the last cut and start cutting a straight line, again stopping approx. 1in from the end of the fabric.

3. Keep working in this way until you have cut the entire rectangle into one continuous strip that you can wind into a ball of yarn.

Cutting larger fabrics into yarn

If you are working with a big piece of fabric such as a sheet or curtain, you can use this fold-and-cut technique on a large floor space to make it quicker and easier. It's useful to try it on some paper first before you start on the fabric.

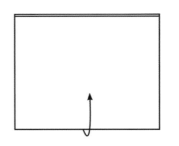
Fig. 2

1. Fold the fabric in half, lifting the bottom edge so that the shorter sides meet at the top.[fig. 2]

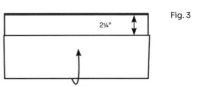
Fig. 3

2. Fold the fabric again, lifting the bottom edge towards the top. This time don't fold it in half—leave approx. 2¼in so it doesn't quite reach the top.[fig. 3]

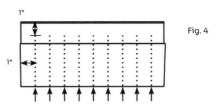
Fig. 4

3. Measure 1in in from the side edge and start cutting in a straight line where the arrows and dotted lines are in the diagram.[fig. 4] Stop when you are approx. 1in away from the top of the fabric. Keep working in this way, measuring 1in from the previous cut and following the dotted lines in the diagram. Make as many cuts as your fabric allows.

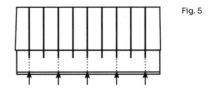
Fig. 5

4. Move to the other side of the fabric so that the folded edge is now at the top. For this step you will only be working through the top layer of the 1in edge left uncut. Cut through the top layer to connect it to the cuts in step 3, cutting only where the dotted lines and arrows are in the diagram.[fig. 5]

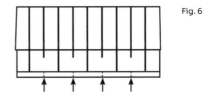
Fig. 6

5. For this step you will only be working through the bottom layer of the 1in edge left uncut. Cut through the bottom layer to connect it to the cuts in step 3, only where the dotted lines and arrows are in the diagram. This should be alternate to the cuts in step 4.[fig. 6]

6. Take one of the edge strips and begin to wind the fabric into a continuous strip that can be wound into a yarn ball.

Stitch
library

Slip rib stitch

This two-color rib stitch uses slip stitch to carry the two colors separately up the work. You will need two colors, color A (navy) and color B (pink). One row in each color is worked throughout. When changing color, twist the yarns together and carry them on the inside of the work. See page 48 for the Escher beanie pattern using this technique.

Worked in the round
With color A, cast on a multiple of 5 sts using the long tail cast on technique. Place a marker and join to work in the round. Work the set-up round, then repeat rounds 1 and 2 to work in slip rib stitch.

Set-up round
With color A, *p2, k3*, repeat section in stars (*) until end of round.

Round 1
With color B, *p2, sl1pwyib, k1, sl1pwyib*, repeat section in stars until end of round.

Round 2
With color A, *p2, k1, sl1pwyib, k1*, repeat section in stars until end of round.

Wavy ribbing stitch

1-color stitch pattern

This wavy stitch pattern cleverly combines garter and rib stitches to create a mock cable texture. See page 52 for the Upstream sweater pattern using this technique.

Worked in the round
Cast on a multiple of 16 sts using the long tail cast on technique. Place a marker and join to work in the round.

Repeat chart to work in wavy ribbing stitch, repeating rounds 1 to 16. See page 154 for chart information and symbols.

Chart

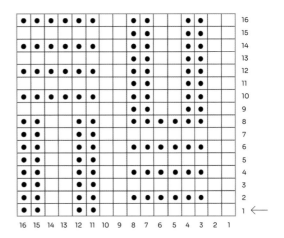

Stranded colorwork stripes

2-color stitch pattern

For this technique, you will be working in stockinette stitch stranded colorwork. One side of the fabric shows vertical stripes, while the other side shows zig-zag floats. Both sides of the fabric are used to create this contrasting stripe pattern. You will need two colors, color A (red) and color B (white). See page 60 for the Static mittens pattern using this technique.

Most patterns and videos advise against crossing the yarns over each other at the back of the work when using two or more colors. This is so that you can easily work in the round in colorwork. However, for this pattern the only way to create the zig-zag floats on one side of the fabric is to cross the yarns over each other when you use them. The yarns will twist together as you knit, but since you are working flat they will untwist after the next row. For more help on this, see crossing yarns on the next page.

Worked flat
With color A, cast on an even number of sts using the cable cast on technique. Repeat steps 1 to 6 to work in stranded colorwork stripes.

1. (RS) *k1b, k1a*, repeat section in stars (*) until end of row.

2. (WS) *p1a, p1b*, repeat section in stars until end of row.

3. Repeat steps 1 and 2 until the striped section measures 1½in, ending with a WS row.

4. (RS) *p1b, p1a*, repeat section in stars until end of row.

5. (WS) *k1a, k1b*, repeat section in stars until end of row.

6. Repeat steps 4 and 5 until the zig-zag section measures 1½in, ending with a WS row.

Crossing yarns on a knit row

Move the color you need to use next over the color you have just used, from right to left, then knit the next st. Work every st in this way, crossing each color over before knitting. [Photos 1 & 2].

Photo 1

Photo 2

Crossing yarns on a purl row

Move the color you need to use next over the color you have just used, from right to left, then purl the next st. Work every st in this way, crossing each color over before purling. [Photos 3 & 4]

Photo 3

Photo 4

Crossing yarns at the start of the row

When you reach a zig-zag float section, cross the yarns at the start of every row to carry the floats right to the edges; this will make seaming neater and less visible. Move the color you need to use first over the other color, so that the yarns twist before starting the first st. [Photos 5 & 6]

Photo 5

Photo 6

Looped stripe stitch

Loops are drawn up and knitted from the garter stitch rows below to create this elongated stitch pattern. You will need two colors, color A (purple) and color B (yellow). Two rows are worked in each color throughout.

When changing color, twist the yarns together and carry them at the side/inside of the work. See page 64 for the Wave vest pattern using this technique.

Worked flat

With color A, cast on a multiple of 6 sts using the cable cast on technique. Work set-up rows 1 and 2, then repeat rows 1 to 4 to work in looped stripe stitch. See the next page for technique help with loop1L and loop1R.

Set-up row 1

(RS) With color B, k all sts.

Set-up row 2

(WS) With color B, k all sts.

Row 1

With color A, k all sts.

Row 2

With color A, k all sts.

Row 3

With color B, *k1, loop1L, k3, loop1R*, repeat section in stars (*) until end of row.

Row 4

With color B, k all sts.

Worked in the round

With color A, cast on a multiple of 6 sts using the long tail cast on technique. Work set-up rounds 1 and 2, then repeat rounds 1 to 4 to work in looped stripe stitch. See the next page for technique help with loop1L and loop1R.

Set-up round 1

With color B, k all sts.

Set-up round 2

With color B, p all sts.

Round 1

With color A, k all sts.

Round 2

With color A, p all sts.

Round 3

With color B, *k1, loop1L, k3, loop1R*,
repeat section in stars until end of row.

Round 4

With color B, p all sts.

Photo 1

Photo 2

Photo 3

Technique help

Loop 1 left (loop1L)

1. Directly below the sts on the left-hand needle,
   you will see a garter st ridge formed in color A,
   then a few rows below it a garter st ridge in
   color B. Follow the second st on the left-hand
   needle down until you get to the color B ridge
   (3 rows below the sts on your needle). This is
   the st highlighted with the arrow.[Photo 1]

Photo 4

2. With your right-hand needle, pick up the
   loop of this st and place it on the right-hand
   needle.[Photos 2 & 3]

3. K1 from the left needle, then pass the loop over
   the st.[Photos 4 & 5]

Photo 5

Technique help

Loop 1 right (loop1R)

1. Directly below the sts on the right-hand
   needle, you will see a garter st ridge formed in
   color A, then a few rows below it a garter st ridge
   in color B. Follow the second st on the right-
   hand needle down until you get to the color B
   ridge (3 rows below the sts on your needle). This
   is the st highlighted with the arrow.[Photo 1]

2. With your left-hand needle, pick up the loop
   of this st, then slip it knitwise onto the right-
   hand needle.[Photos 2, 3 & 4]

3. K1 from the left-hand needle, then pass the loop
   over the st.[Photos 5 & 6]

Photo 1

Photo 2

Photo 3

Photo 4

Photo 5

Photo 6

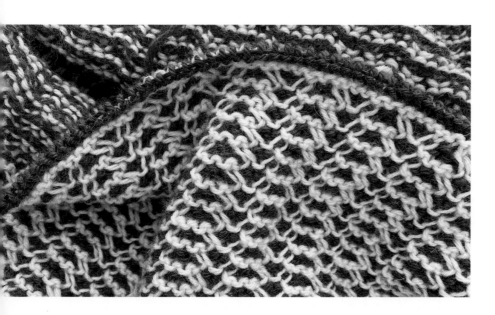

Garter rib stitch

In this rib pattern, garter stitch replaces the traditional purl stitches, while a central slip stitch in the knit stitches carries the two colors side by side up the rib. You will need two colors, color A (burgundy) and color B (green).
One row in each color is worked throughout.

When changing color, twist the yarns together and carry them on the inside of the work.
See page 64 for the Wave vest pattern using this technique.

Worked in the round
With color A, cast on a multiple of 6 sts using the long tail cast on technique. Place a marker and join to work in the round. Work set-up rounds 1 and 2, then repeat rounds 1 and 2 to work in garter rib stitch.

Set-up round 1
With color A, *k3, p3*, repeat section in stars (*) until end of round.

Set-up round 2
With color B, *sl1pwyib, k1, sl1pwyib, p3*, repeat section in stars until end of round.

Round 1
With color A, *k1, sl1pwyib, k1, k3*, repeat section in stars until end of round.

Round 2
With color B, *sl1pwyib, k1, sl1pwyib, p3*, repeat section in stars until end of round.

Pillar and web stitch

The structured vertical pillars and open webs in this stitch are created using two different needle sizes, and instead of yarn overs it uses a purl over technique. See page 74 for the Scribble top pattern using this technique.

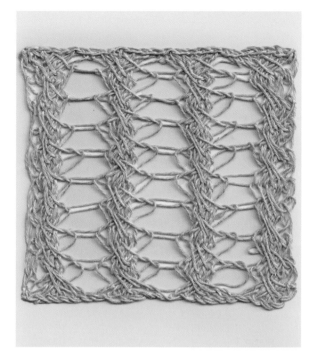

Worked flat

Use two needle sizes, one double the size of the other; we are using US 8 (5mm) and US 15 (10mm).
Cast on a multiple of 6 + 2 sts using US 8 (5mm) needles and the cable cast on technique.
Repeat rows 1 and 2 to work in pillar and web stitch.
See Technique Help on the next page for help with sk3, p3 over, p3.

Row 1

(RS) Using a US 15 (10mm) needle, k all sts.

Row 2

(WS) Using a US 8 (5mm) needle, p1, *sk3, p3 over, p3*, repeat section in stars (*) until 1 st remains, p1.

Technique help

sk3, p3 over, p3:

1. Skip the first 3 sts on your left-hand needle, insert the tip of your right-hand needle purlwise into the 4th st on the left-hand needle, complete a p st. [Photos 1, 2 & 3]

2. Draw the st you have just purled over the 3 skipped sts and off the left-hand needle onto the right-hand needle. [Photos 4, 5 & 6]

3. You have now completed 1 purl over. Repeat steps 1 and 2 twice more so you have purled 3 sts in total over the 3 skipped sts. [Photo 7]

4. Now purl the 3 skipped sts on your left-hand needle as normal. [Photo 8]

Photo 1

Photo 2

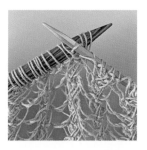

Photo 3

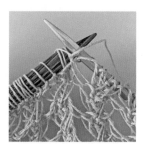

Photo 4

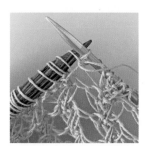

Photo 5

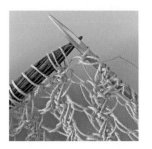

Photo 6

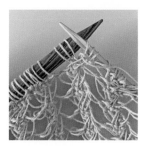

Photo 7

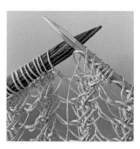

Photo 8

Zig-zag jacquard stitch

This two-color textured stitch is made by bringing the yarn across the front of the work when slipping multiple stitches, creating a visible strand called a float. You will need two colors, color A (gray) and color B (orange). Six rows are worked in each color throughout. When a color is not in use, carry it up the side of the work. See page 84 for the Rush hood pattern using this technique.

Worked flat
With color A, cast on a multiple of 8 + 2 sts using the cable cast on technique. Work set-up rows 1 and 2, then repeat rows 1 to 12 to work in zig-zag jacquard stitch.

Set-up row 1
(RS) With color A, k all sts.

Set-up row 2
(WS) P all sts.

Row 1
With color B, k1, *sl4p, k4*, repeat section in stars (*) until 1 st remains, k1.

Row 2
P1, *p3, sl4pwyib, p1*, repeat section in stars until 1 st remains, p1.

Row 3
K1, *k2, sl4p, k2*, repeat section in stars until 1 st remains, k1.

Row 4
P1, *p1, sl4pwyib, p3* repeat section in stars until 1 st remains, p1.

Row 5
K1, *k4, sl4p* repeat section in stars until 1 st remains, k1.

Row 6
P1, *sl3pwyib, p4, sl1pwyib*, repeat section in stars until 1 st remains, p1.

Row 7
With color A, k1, *k1, sl4p, k3*, repeat section in stars until 1 st remains, k1.

Row 8
P1, *p4, sl4pwyib*, repeat section in stars until 1 st remains, p1.

Row 9
K1, *sl3p, k4, sl1p*, repeat section in stars until 1 st remains, k1.

Row 10
P1, *sl2pwyib, p4, sl2pwyib*, repeat section in stars until 1 st remains, p1.

Row 11
K1, *sl1p, k4, sl3p*, repeat section in stars until 1 st remains, k1.

Row 12
P1, *sl4pwyib, p4*, repeat section in stars until 1 st remains, p1.

Textured floats

Rush hood

Long slip stripe stitch

The elongated stitches that overlay the stripes in this stitch are created using slip stitches.

We have used four colors, color A (gray), color B (beige), color C (blue), and color D (green), along with a mix of yarn weights to exaggerate the texture.

When changing color, twist the yarns together and carry them up the side or inside of the work. See page 94 for the Ziggy sweater pattern using this technique.

Worked flat

With color A, cast on an odd number of sts using the cable cast on technique. Work the set-up row, then repeat steps 1 to 7 to work in long slip stripe stitch.

Set-up row

(RS) With color A, k all sts.

1. (WS) With color B, *p1, sl1p*, repeat section in stars (*) until 1 st remains, p1.

2. (RS) *K1, sl1pwyib*, repeat section in stars until 1 st remains, k1.

3. Repeat step 1 once more.

4. K 1 row.

5. With color C, repeat steps 1 to 4 once more.

6. With color D, repeat steps 1 to 4 once more.

7. With color A, repeat steps 1 to 4 once more.

Mixed yarn weights   Ziggy sweater

Worked in the round

With color A, cast on an even number of sts using the long tail cast on technique. Place a marker and join to work in the round. Work the set-up round, then repeat steps 1 to 6 to work in long slip stripe stitch.

Set-up round

With color A, k all sts.

1. With color B, *k1, sl1pwyib*, repeat section in stars (*) until end of round.

2. Repeat step 1 twice more.

3. K 1 round.

4. With color C, repeat steps 1 to 3 once more.

5. With color D, repeat steps 1 to 3 once more.

6. With color A, repeat steps 1 to 3 once more.

Striped slip rib stitch

Worked in a rib pattern, this stitch is made up of vertical stripes of slip stitches and purl sections. Two colors alternate throughout to achieve the mix of colors on every row. We have worked this stitch in color blocks using three colors, color A (navy), color B (green), and color C (white). See page 104 for the Off grid top pattern using this technique.

Worked flat

With color A, cast on a multiple of 14 + 3 sts using the long tail cast on technique. Work the set-up row, then repeat steps 1 to 4 to work in striped slip rib stitch. Use two double-pointed needles or circular needles so you can change color every row without cutting the yarns. After 4 repeats (16 rows in total), we swapped color B for color C.

Set-up row

(WS) With color A, *k3, p3, k3, p1, k1, p1, k1, p1*, repeat section in stars (*) until 3 sts remain, k3.

Row 1

(RS) With color B, *p3, k1, p1, sl1pwyib, p1, k1, p3, k1, sl1pwyib, k1*, repeat section in stars until 3 sts remain, p3. Slide sts to the other end of the needle to work color A next.

Row 2

(RS) With color A, *p3, sl1pwyib, p1, k1, p1, sl1pwyib, p3, k3*, repeat section in stars until 3 sts remain, p3.

Row 3

(WS) With color B, *k3, p1, sl1p, p1, k3, p1, k1, sl1p, k1, p1*, repeat section in stars until 3 sts remain, k3. Slide sts to the other end of the needle to work color A next.

Row 4

(WS) With color A, *k3, p3, k3, sl1p, k1, p1, k1, sl1p*, repeat section in stars until 3 sts remain, k3.

Worked in the round

With color A, cast on a multiple of 14 sts using the long tail cast on technique. Place a marker and join to work in the round. Work the set-up round, then repeat steps 1 and 2 to work in striped slip rib stitch. After 8 repeats (16 rounds in total), we swapped color B for color C.

Set-up round

With color A, *p3, k1, p1, k1, p1, k1, p3, k3*, repeat section in stars (*) until end of round.

Round 1

With color B, *p3, k1, p1, sl1pwyib, p1, k1, p3, k1, sl1pwyib, k1*, repeat section in stars until end of round.

Round 2

With color A, *p3, sl1pwyib, p1, k1, p1, sl1pwyib, p3, k3*, repeat section in stars until end of round.

Basket rib stitch

This three-color stitch pattern is achieved by using alternate elongated slip stitches. You will need three colors, color A (brown), color B (white), and color C (blue). One row in each color is worked throughout. When changing color, there is no need to cut the yarns—the correct color should be waiting at the end of each row. See page 112 for the Echo scarf pattern using this technique.

Worked flat

With color A, cast on a multiple of 2 + 3 sts using the long tail cast on technique.

Work the set-up row, then repeat rows 1 to 4 to work in basket rib stitch. When repeating rows 1 to 4, ignore the color instructions; instead, make sure you keep in sequence working 1 row in each color throughout.

Set-up row

(WS) With color A, sl1p, p all sts.

Row 1

(RS) With color B, *sl1pwyib, k1*, repeat section in stars (*) until 1 st remains, k1.

Row 2

With color C, *sl1p, k1*, repeat section in stars until 1 st remains, p1.

Row 3

With color A, sl1pwyib, k all sts.

Row 4

With color B, sl1p, p all sts.

Twisted woven stitch

The woven texture of this stitch is achieved by working into the row below, creating a tight knit structure. We suggest keeping the gauge on the working yarn slightly loose while working this stitch to make it as comfortable as possible. See page 124 for the Helix bag pattern using this technique.

Worked flat

Cast on any number of sts using the long tail cast on technique. Work the set-up row, then repeat rows 1 and 2 to work in twisted woven stitch. See Technique Help on page 42 for further help on this stitch.

Set-up row
(WS) P all sts.

Row 1
(RS) k1, *between the next 2 sts on the left needle, pick up and k1 from the row below, sl1pwyib*, repeat section in stars (*) until 1 st remains, k1.

Row 2
(WS) P1, *p2tog*, repeat section in stars until 1 st remains, p1.

Worked in the round

Cast on any number of sts using the long tail cast on technique. Work the set-up round, then repeat rounds 1 and 2 to work in twisted woven stitch.

Set-up round
K all sts.

Round 1
Between the next 2 sts on the left needle, pick up and k1 from the row below, sl1pwyib, repeat section in stars (*) until end of round.

Round 2
k2tog repeat section in stars until end of round.

Technique help

Between the next 2 sts on the left needle, pick up and k1 from the row below, sl1pwyib:

1. Between the next 2 sts on the left needle, insert the right needle into the row below.[Photos 1 & 2]

2. Wrap the working yarn around the right needle [Photo 3] and draw the yarn through the work, completing a k st.[Photo 4]

3. Keeping the yarn at the back of the work, slip the first st on the left needle purlwise, moving it to the right needle.[Photos 5 & 6]

Photo 1

Photo 2

Photo 3

Photo 4

Photo 5

Photo 6

Knit

Irregular cable stitch

This cable pattern incorporates a variety of cable crosses to move the stitches in a seemingly irregular way. The pattern is even more exaggerated when using a thicker yarn. See page 128 for the Drift jacket pattern using this technique.

Worked flat

Cast on a multiple of 21 + 3 sts using the long tail cast on technique. Work the set-up row, then repeat rows 1 to 36 of the chart to work the irregular cable. See page 154 for chart information and symbols.

Set-up row

(WS) k3 *p3, k3, p6, k3, p3, k3*, repeat section in stars (*) until end of row.

Chart

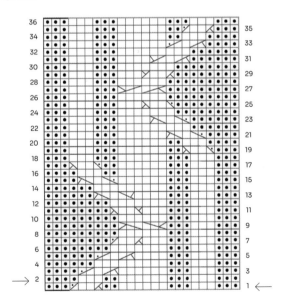

Garter stripe stitch

In this graphic contrast pattern, vertical stripes of slip stiches interplay with sections of garter stitch. Two colors alternate throughout to achieve the mix of colors on every row.

We have worked this stitch in color blocks using three colors, color A (gray), color B (cream), and color C (brown). See page 142 for the Anni cloth set pattern using this technique.

Worked flat
With color A, cast on a multiple of 10 + 8 sts using the cable cast on technique. Work the set-up row, then repeat rows 1 to 4 to work in garter stripe stitch. Use two double-pointed needles or circular needles so you can change color every row without cutting the yarns. After 5 repeats (20 rows in total), we swapped color B for color C.

Set-up row
(RS) With color A, k all sts. Turn work.

Row 1
(WS) With color B, k8, *p1, sl1p, k8*, repeat section in stars (*) until end of row. Slide sts to the other end of the needles.

Row 2
(WS) With color A, p8, *sl1p, p9*, repeat section in stars until end of row. Turn work.

Row 3
(RS) With color B, p8, *sl1pwyib, k1, p8*, repeat section in stars until end of row. Slide sts to the other end of the needles.

Row 4
(RS) With color A, k8, *k1, sl1pwyib, k8*, repeat section in stars until end of row. Turn work.

Double linen stitch

This three-color, checked linen stitch is made by slipping two stitches while the yarn remains at the front of the work, creating a visible strand called a float. You will need three colors, color A (bronze), color B (white), and color C (pink). One row is worked in each color throughout.

When changing color, there is no need to cut the yarns—the correct color should be waiting at the end of each row. See page 142 for the Anni cloth set pattern using this technique.

Worked flat
With color A, cast on a multiple of 4 sts using the long tail cast on technique. Work the set-up row, then repeat rows 1 and 2 to work in double linen stitch. Keep in sequence, working 1 row in colors A, B, and C throughout.

Set-up row
(WS) WIth color A, p all sts.

Row 1
(RS) With next color, k1, *sl2p, k2*, repeat section in stars (*) until 3 sts remain, sl2p, k1.

Row 2
(WS) With next color, p3, *sl2pwyib, p2*, repeat section in stars until 1 st remains, p1.

Patterns

Slip rib stitch

Escher beanie

Knitted in a two-color slip rib stitch, the Escher beanie is worked in the round from the bottom up, alternating between color A and color B rounds. The folded hem is worked first, followed by the main section of the beanie where the stitch is reversed to show the right side of the stitch when the hem is folded up.

Size

This pattern includes 2 sizes:

Size 1: to fit head circumference 21–23in

Size 2: to fit head circumference 23–25in

When the instructions differ between sizes, they will be written as follows: size 1 [size 2].

Flat measurements (unfolded)

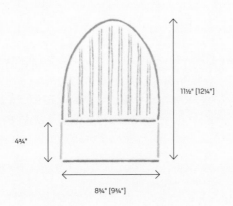

11½" [12¼"]

4¾"

8¾" [9¾"]

Yarn

Worsted weight yarn. You will need approx. 130yds/119m [168yds/154m] of color A and 100yds/91m [138yds/126m] of color B.

We used

Color A - Brown

2 balls of BC Garn, Semilla Grosso in Dark Brown – 100% organic wool (87yds/80m per 50g ball)

Color B - Blue

2 balls of Kremke Soul Wool, The Merry Merino 70 in color 21 – 100% wool (77yds/70m per 50g ball)

In the yellow-and-white sample, we used Fonty Tartan 6 in colors 2022 and 2025

Alternative yarn suggestions: Drops Alaska, Drops Nepal, Lana Grossa Bingo

Recommended needles

US 8 (5mm) circular needles, length 16–20in.

Gauge

Slip rib stitch after blocking (see page 24):

4 x 4in = 21 stitches x 32 rows

Instructions

1. Cast on 95 [105] sts using color A and the long tail cast on technique.

   Place marker and join to work in the round, being careful not to twist your sts.

2. *K3, p2*, repeat section in stars (*) until end of round.

3. With color B, *sl1pwyib, k1, sl1pwyib, p2*, repeat section in stars until end of round.

4. With color A, *k1, sl1pwyib, k1, p2*, repeat section in stars until end of round.

5. Repeat steps 3 and 4 until your piece measures 4¾in from the cast-on edge (approx. 35 more rounds), ending with a color B round. You have now knitted the fold-up section of the beanie.

6. You will now be working back across the sts you have just worked. To do this, turn your work—the last st worked should now be on your left-hand needle, ready to work again. Work across the sts as follows: With color A, *p2, k1, sl1pwyib, k1*, repeat section in stars until end of round.

7. You will now continue to work in the round this way, keeping the yarn at the back of the work when not in use. With color B, *p2, sl1pwyib, k1, sl1pwyib*, repeat section in stars until end of round.

8. With color A, *p2, k1, sl1pwyib, k1*, repeat section in stars until end of round.

9. Repeat steps 7 and 8 until your piece measures 10¾in [11½in] from the cast-on edge (approx. 47 [53] more rounds), ending with a color B round.

10. With color A, *p2, k1, sl1pwyib, k1, p2tog, k1, sl1pwyib, k1*, repeat section in stars until 5 sts remain, p2, k1, sl1pwyib, k1. (86 [95] sts.)

11. With color B, *p2, sl1pwyib, k1, sl1pwyib, p1, sl1pwyib, k1, sl1pwyib*, repeat section in stars until 5 sts remain, p2, sl1pwyib, k1, sl1pwyib.

12. With color A, *p2tog, k1, sl1pwyib, k1, p1, k1, sl1pwyib, k1*, repeat section in stars until 5 sts remain, p2tog, k1, sl1pwyib, k1. (76 [84] sts.)

13. With color B, *p1, sl1pwyib, ssk, repeat section in stars until end of round. (57 [63] sts.)

14. With color A, *CDD* repeat section in stars until end of round. (19 [21] sts.) At this point your sts can be harder to knit, so you may need to use the magic loop technique of knitting in the round.

15. Cut the yarn leaving a 6in yarn tail and thread a tapestry needle with the yarn tail. Starting with first st of the round, insert needle through each of the sts. Remove needles and pull on the yarn tail to close up the top of the hat. Secure yarn inside hat and weave in any loose ends.

   We recommend that you block your beanie to achieve the correct measurements.

See page 15 for how to knit the Escher beanie in intersecting stripes using leftover yarn.

Upstream sweater

Knitted in wavy ribbing stitch, the Upstream sweater is designed with long raglan sleeves and a high ribbed neck. Knitted in the round from the top down, the pattern starts with the 2 x 2 rib neck and then changes to wavy ribbing stitch. Short rows are worked at the bottom of the neck to add shaping. Increases are made at the four raglan points until the armholes are reached. The stitches are then divided into the body and two sleeves and worked separately in the round, changing to 2 x 2 rib when reaching the hem and cuff.

Size

This pattern includes 7 sizes. When the instructions differ between sizes, they will be written as follows: size 1 [size 2, size 3, sizes 4-5, size 6, size 7, size 8]. See page 150 for size chart. Iris and Lydia wear size 2. If you are in between sizes 1 and 2 or sizes 5 and 6, we suggest you go up a size. If you are in between sizes 2 and 3, we suggest you go down a size unless you want a more oversized fit.

Flat measurements

Below rib: 8¼" [8¼", 8¼", 8¾", 8¾", 9½", 9½"]

25½" [26½", 26½", 27½", 27½", 28½", 28½"]

4"

7" [8¼", 9½", 9½", 11", 11", 12½"]

6½" [8½", 10", 11¾", 14", 16", 15¾"]

24¾"[24¾", 24¾", 24¾", 25¾", 25¾", 26"]

5" [5", 5", 5½", 5½", 6¼", 6¼"]

1¾"

1¾"

16½" [19¾", 21¾", 24½", 27¼", 30", 30"]

Yarn

Worsted weight yarn. Approx. 191yds/175m per 100g. You will need approx. 1283yds/1173m [1436yds/1313m, 1627yds/1488m, 1799yds/1645m, 2067yds/1890m, 2201yds/2013m, 2297yds/2100m].

We used

7 [8, 9, 10, 11, 12, 13] balls of By Laxtons Sheepsoft Aran in Bishopdale – 100% wool (191yds/175m per 100g ball)

In the Green sample, we used Cascade 220 Aran in color 1034
Alternative yarn suggestions: Rico Essentials Soft Merino Aran, West Yorkshire Spinners The Croft Shetland Aran, Drops Nepal

Recommended needles

US 4 (3.5mm) circular knitting needles, length 16–20in and 32in
US 7 (4.5mm) circular knitting needles, length 16–20in and 32–47in.

Gauge

Wavy ribbing stitch (see page 25) after blocking on US 7 (4.5mm) needles:
4 x 4in = 23 stitches x 28 rows

Knitting notes

- You will need four stitch markers, placed in this formation according to step 2:

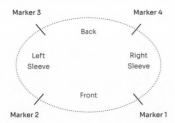

- Increases for the raglan are made before and after each marker according to the pattern.
- Please refer to the wavy ribbing stitch chart on page 25 when referenced in the instructions. If you are instructed to start with a certain stitch in the stitch pattern, work from that stitch to the end of the chart, then start again at stitch 1 and work full repeats to the end of the round.

- Please refer to the raglan charts on pages 156–9 when referenced in the instructions.
- **German short row turns:** When told to turn in step 13, to keep the short rows neat work a German short row turn as follows:
1. Turn the work: If you are on a RS row and turn the work, make sure yarn is at WS of work; if you are on a WS row and turn the work, make sure yarn is at RS of work.
2. Turning st = slip the first stitch purlwise, bring the working yarn up and over the needle, pulling tightly so that both strands of the slipped stitch go over the needle. Holding the yarn tightly, continue working according to the pattern.
3. When working back across this turning stitch, it will look like a double stitch—make sure you work both strands together as one stitch.

Wavy ribbing stitch

Instructions

1. With US 4 (3.5mm) needles, length 16–20in, cast on 96 [96, 96, 104, 104, 112, 112] sts using the long tail cast on technique.

   Place marker 1 and join to work in the round. This marker should be different to the other markers to show the start of the round.

2. *K2, p2 [p2, p2, p3, p3, p4, p4], (k2, p2) x7, p0 [p0, p0, p1, p1, p2, p2], place marker 2, k2, p2 [p2, p2, p3, p3, p4, p4], (k2, p2) x3, p0 [p0, p0, p1, p1, p2, p2]*, place marker 3. Repeat section in stars (*) once more placing marker 4.

Sizes 1, 2 and 3 only:

3. *K2, p2*, repeat section in stars until end of round.

Sizes 4-5, 6, 7 and 8 only:

4. *K2, [p3, p3, p4, p4], (k2, p2) x7, [p1, p1, p2, p2], k2, [p3, p3, p4, p4], (k2, p2) x3, [p1, p1, p2, p2]*, repeat section in stars once more.

All sizes:

5. Repeat step 3 [3, 3, 4, 4, 4, 4] until your piece measures 1¾in from the cast-on edge.

Sizes 1, 2 and 3 only:

6. With US 7 (4.5mm) needles, length 16–20in work rounds 1 to 12 of the wavy ribbing st chart (see page 25).

Sizes 4-5, 6, 7 and 8 only:

7. With US 7 (4.5mm) needles, length 16–20in, *k2, [p1, p1, p2, p2] starting with st 3 on the chart, work round 1 of the wavy ribbing

st chart twice, [p1, p1, p2, p2], slip marker, k2, [p1, p1, p2, p2] starting with st 3 on the chart, work round 1 of the wavy ribbing st chart once, [p1, p1, p2, p2], slip marker.* Repeat section in stars once more.

8. Repeat step 7 working rounds 2 to 12 of the wavy ribbing st chart. Work the same way as step 7 but substitute 'work round 1' with whichever round you are on.

All sizes:

9. You will now work the first raglan increases, which will sit on the neck as follows: *m1R, slip marker, k2, m1L, starting with st 3 [3, 3, 2, 2, 1, 1] on the chart, repeat round 13 of the wavy ribbing st chart until you reach next marker.* Repeat section in stars a further 3 times. (104 [104, 104, 112, 112, 120, 120sts.)

10. *K2, starting with st 2 [2, 2, 1, 1, 16, 16] on the chart, work round 14 of the wavy ribbing st chart until you reach next marker.* Repeat section in stars a further 3 times.

11. *M1R, slip marker, k2, m1L, starting with st 2 [2, 2, 1, 1, 16, 16] on the chart, work round 15 of the wavy ribbing st chart until you reach next marker.* Repeat section in stars a further 3 times. (112 [112, 112, 120, 120, 128, 128] sts.)

12. *K2, starting with st 1 [1, 1, 16, 16, 15, 15] on the chart, work round 16 of the wavy ribbing st chart until you reach next marker.* Repeat section in stars a further 3 times.

13. In this step you will work the short rows to shape the neck whille still increasing for the raglan as follows:

Set up = slip marker, k4 [k4, k4, k5, k5, k6, k2], p2, k1 [k1, k0, k0, k0, k0, k1]. Turn work. (See notes on German short row turn.)

Row 1: (WS) Turning st, k2 [k2, kl, k1, k1, k1, k0], p4 [p4, p4, p5, p5, p6, p4], slip marker, k0 [k0, k0, k1, k1, k2, k2], *p10, k2, p2, k2*, p4 [p4, p4, p5, p5, p6, p6], slip marker, k0 [k0, k0, k1, k1, k2, k2], repeat section in stars twice more. P4 [p4, p4, p5, p5, p6, p6], slip marker, k0 [k0, k0, k1, k1, k2, k2], repeat section in stars once more, p4 [p4, p4, p5, p5, p6, p6], slip marker, k0 [k0, k0, k1, k1, k2, k2], p5 [p5, p4, p4, p4, p4, p1]. Turn work.

Row 2: (RS) Turning st, p2 [p2, p1, p1, p1, p1, p2], k2 [k2, k2, k2, k2, k2, k0], p0 [p0, p0, p1, p1, p2, p0], *m1R, slip marker, k2, m1L, p0 [p0, p0, p1, p1, p2, p2], work row 16 of the wavy ribbing st chart until you reach next marker.* Repeat section in stars a further 2 times. M1R, slip marker, k2, m1L, p0 [p0, p0, p0, p1, p1, p2, p2], k2, p2 [p2, p2, p2, p2, p2, p1], k2 [k2, k2, k2, k2, k2, k0], p2 [p2, p1, p1, p1, p1, p0], k2 [k2, k0, k0, k0, k0, k0] remembering to work the 2 strands of the turning st together. Turn work. (120 [120, 120, 128, 128, 136, 136] sts.)

Row 3: (WS) Turning st, p1 [p1, p2, p2, p2, p2, p7], k2 [k2, k2, k2, k2, k2, k0], p2 [p2, p3, p3, p3, p3, p0], k2 [k2, k0, k0, k0, k0, k0], p5 [p5, p2, p3, p3, p4, p0], slip marker, p0 [p0, p0, p0, p0, p1, p1], k1 [k1, k1, k2, k2, k2, k2], *p10, k2, p2, k2*, p5 [p5, p5, p6, p6, p7, p7], slip marker, p0 [p0, p0, p0, p0, p1, p1], k1 [k1, k1, k2, k2, k2, k2], repeat section in stars twice more. P5 [p5, p5, p6, p6, p7, p7], slip marker, p0 [p0, p0, p0, p0, p1], k1

[k1, k1, k2, k2, k2, k2], repeat section in stars once more. P5 [p5, p5, p6, p6, p7, p7], slip marker, p0 [p0, p0, p0, p0, p1, p1], k1 [k1, k1, k2, k2, k2, k2], p10 [p10, p7, p7, p7, p7, p3] remembering to work the 2 strands of the turning st together. Turn work.

Row 4: (RS) Turning st, k1 [k1, k0, k0, k0, k0, k0], p6 [p6, p4, p4, p4, p4, p0], k2, p1 [p1, p1, p2, p2, p2, p2], k0 [k0, k0, k0, k0, k1, k1], *m1R, slip marker, k2, m1L, k0 [k0, k0, k0, k0, k1, k1], p1 [p1, p1, p2, p2, p2, p2], work row 16 of the wavy ribbing st chart until you reach next marker.* Repeat section in stars a further 2 times. M1R, slip marker, k2, m1L, k0 [k0, k0, k0, k0, k1, k1], p0 [p0, p1, p2, p2, p2, p2], k0 [k0, k2, k2, k2, k2, k2], p0 [p0, p2, p2, p2, p2, p2], k0 [k0, k2, k2, k2, k2, k2], p0 [p0, p2, p2, p2, p2, p0], k0 [k0, k2, k2, k2, k2, k0], remembering to work the 2 strands of the turning st together. For sizes 3 to 8, turn work and go to Row 5. For sizes 1 and 2 skip to step 14. (128 [128, 128, 136, 136, 144, 144] sts.)

Row 5: (WS) Turning st, p1, k2, p2, [k2, k2, k2, k2, k0], [p6, p7, p7, p8, p6], slip marker, [p0, p1, p1, p2, p2], k2, *p10, k2, p2, k2*, [p6, p7, p7, p8, p8], slip marker, [p0, p1, p1, p2, p2], k2, repeat section in stars twice more. [P6, p7, p7, p8, p8], slip marker, [p0, p1, p1, p2, p2], k2, repeat section in stars once more. [P6, p7, p7, p8, p8], slip marker, [p0, p1, p1, p2, p2], k2, [p10, p10, p10, p10, p6] remembering to work the 2 strands of the turning st together. Turn work.

Row 6: (RS) Turning st, [k1, k1, k1, k1, k0], [p6, p6, p6, p6, p3], k2, p2, [k0, k1, k1, k2, k2], *m1R, slip marker, k2, m1L, [k0, k1, k1, k2, k2], p2, work row 16 of the wavy ribbing st chart until you reach next marker.* Repeat section in stars a further 2 times. M1R, slip marker, k2, m1L. [k0, k0, k0, k0, k2], [p0 p0, p0, p0, p2], [k0, k0, k0, k0, k2], [p0, p0, p0, p0, p2], [k0, k0, k0, k0, k2], [p0 p0, p0, p0, p2], [k0, k0, k0, k0, k1], remembering to work the 2 strands of the turning st together. For size 8, turn work and go to Row 7. For sizes 3 to 7, skip to step 14. ([136, 144, 144, 152, 152] sts.)

Row 7: (WS) Turning st, k2, p2, k2, p9, slip marker, k1, p2, k2, *p10, k2, p2, k2*, p9, slip marker, k1, p2, k2, repeat section in stars twice more. P9, slip marker, k1, p2, k2, repeat section in stars once more. P9, slip marker, k1, p2, k2, p9, remembering to work the 2 strands of the turning st together. Turn work.

Row 8: (RS) Turning st, p6, k2, p2, k2, p1, *m1R, slip marker, k2, m1L, p1, k2, p2, work row 16 of the wavy ribbing st chart until you reach next marker.* Repeat section in stars a further 2 times. M1R, slip marker, k2, m1L. (160 sts.)

14. You should have just gone past marker 1 (start of the round.) Slip 3 sts from right needle back to left needle to start working in the round continuously again. You may need to break the yarn and re-join. *K2 [k2, k3, k4, k4, k2, k2], p2 [p2, p2, p2, p2, p1, p2], k0 [k0, k0, k0, k0, k2, k2], p0 [p0, p0, p0, p0, p2, p2], work round 1 of the wavy ribbing st chart until you reach next marker.* Remember to work the 2 strands of the turning st together. Repeat section in stars a further 3 times.

15. Work rounds 1 to 32 of the raglan chart 1 [1, 2, 2, 2, 2, 3] time(s). Follow only the chart for your size. As the sts increase, at some point you will need to swap to US 7 (4.5mm) needles, length 32–47in. (256 [256, 392, 400, 400, 408, 544] sts.)

Sizes 1, 2, 3, 4–5, 6 and 7 only:

16. Work rounds 1 to 13 [27, 7, 3, 19, 17] of the raglan chart. (312 [368, 424, 416, 480, 480] sts.)

Sizes 4–5, 6, 7 and 8 only:

17. Work rounds 1 to [16, 16, 32, 15] of the front/back and sleeve charts. ([448, 512, 544, 576] sts.)

All sizes:

18. Now it's time to divide the sts into the body and the two sleeves:

Work row 14 [28, 8, 20, 4, 18, 16] of the raglan chart across the front until you reach next marker. Remove marker, place next 70 [84, 98, 96, 112, 112, 128] sts (all sts until you reach next marker) on a st holder for one sleeve. Remove next marker, cast on 10 [12, 14, 16, 16, 16, 16] sts on the right needle using the cable cast on technique; this is for the underarm. Join cast-on sts with the back and repeat the section in stars once more.

Join cast-on sts to the front, k1 [k2, k0, k0, k0, k0, k0], p2 [p0, p1, p0, p0, p0, p0], then place marker to show start of round. You will now work the body in the round. (192 [224, 256, 288, 320, 352, 352] sts.)

19. Work rounds 8 [14, 2, 6, 14, 4, 2] to 16 of the wavy ribbing st chart.

20. Repeat rounds 1 to 16 of the wavy ribbing st chart until body measures 23in [23in, 23in, 23in, 24in, 24in, 24in] from the cast-on neck edge (measure on the front). Make sure last row is either row 8 or row 16, (approx. 5 [4.5, 3, 2.5, 2.5, 1, 1] repeats).

21. With US 4 (3.5mm) needles, length 32in, *k2, p2*, repeat section in stars until end of round.

22. Repeat step 21 until 2 x 2 rib measures 1¾in.

23. Bind off in ribbing.

    The body is now complete. You will now work the sleeve sts put on st holders in step 18.

24. Place sts from one sleeve on your US 7 (4.5mm) needles, length 16–20in. RS facing outwards, pick up and k 10 [12, 14, 16, 16, 16, 16] sts along the sts cast on for the body underarm, place marker after picking up 5 [6, 7, 8, 8, 8, 8] of the 10 [12, 14, 16, 16, 16, 16] sts to mark the underarm point.

    You will now work in the round over these 80 [96, 112, 112, 128, 128, 144] sts. K1 [k2, k0, k0, k0, k0, k0], p2 [p0, p1, p0, p0, p0, p0], then work round 7 [13, 1, 5, 13, 3, 1] of the wavy ribbing st chart until you reach the underarm marker.

25. Work rounds 16 [6, 10, 14, 6, 12, 10] to 16 of the wavy ribbing st chart. (1 [11, 7, 3, 11, 5, 7] rounds.)

26. Repeat rounds 1 to 16 of the wavy ribbing st chart a further 6 [3, 1, 2, 1, 1, 1] times. (96 [48, 16, 32, 16, 16, 16] rounds.)

27. You will now start decreasing until you reach the sleeve cuff. Keep repeating rounds 1 to 16 of the wavy ribbing st chart, keeping in pattern while decreasing as instructed.

    K2, k2tog, work in pattern until 2 sts remain, ssk. (78 [94, 110, 110, 126, 126, 142] sts.)

28. Work 6 [4, 3, 3, 1, 2, 1] rounds in pattern.

29. K2, k2tog, work in pattern until 2 sts remain, ssk. (76 [92, 108, 108, 124, 124, 140 sts.)

30. **All sizes:**
    Repeat steps 28 to 29 a further 2 [10, 18, 14, 22, 17, 26] times. (72 [72, 72, 80, 80, 90, 88] sts.)

    At this point you should have worked 1 [3, 4, 3, 2, 3, 3] full repeats of the wavy ribbing st chart and repeated rounds 1 to 6 [8, 13, 13, 15, 7, 7] once more from step 27.

    Sizes 1, 3, 4–5, 6 and 8 only:
31. Work 2 [3, 3, 9, 1] rounds in pattern, finishing on row 8 [16, 16, 8, 8] of the wavy ribbing st chart.

    Size 7 only:
32. Repeat step 29 once more. (88 sts.)

All sizes:

33. Using US 4 (3.5mm) needles, length 16–20in, *k2, p2*, repeat section in stars until end of round.

34. Repeat step 33 until 2 x 2 rib measures 1¾in.

35. Bind off in ribbing.

36. Repeat steps 24 to 35 for the other sleeve.

37. Weave in loose ends. We recommend you block your sweater to achieve the correct measurements.

This is our very first top-down, seamless sweater design. I've been slightly scared of this method of knitting for so long, but it's such a joy!

Static
mittens

The Static mittens use the stranded colorwork stripes technique, alternating colors every stitch to create an all-over illusive pattern. The mittens are knitted flat from the wrist cuff to the top of the mitten, then seamed down one side. When the base of the thumb is reached, stitches are increased and the thumb is finished before knitting the remainder of the mitten. See page 26 for stitch information before you start.

Size
One size

Flat measurements

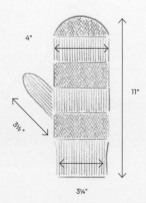

4"

11"

3½"

3¼"

Yarn
DK weight yarn. You will need approx. 131yds/120m per color.

We used
Color A – Purple
   1 ball of Lang Yarns Merino 120 in color 0380 – 100% Merino wool (131yds/120m per 50g ball)
Color B – White
   1 ball of By Laxtons Sheepsoft DK in Airedale – 100% British wool (240yds/220m per 100g ball)
Alternative yarn suggestions: Rico Essentials Merino DK, Sandnes Garn Double Sunday, Drops Merino Extra Fine, Drops Karisma

Recommended needles
US 6 (4mm) knitting needles

Gauge
Stranded colorwork stripes (see page 26) after blocking: 4 x 4in = 26 stitches x 26 rows

Stranded colorwork stripes

Instructions

Follow the instructions twice to make the left and right mittens.

1. With color A, cast on 46 sts using the long tail cast on technique.

2. (WS) *p1a, p1b*, repeat section in stars (*) until end of row.

3. *K1b, k1a*, repeat section in stars until end of row.

4. Repeat steps 2 and 3 until your piece measures 3¼in from the cast-on edge (approx. 19 more rows), ending with a WS row.

5. (RS) p1b, p1a, *p1b, p1a, p1b, p1a, p1b, p1a, p1b, p1a, m1pb, p1a, m1pb, p1a, p1b, p1a, p1b, p1a, p1b, p1a, p1b, m1pa, p1b, m1pa*. Repeat section in stars once more. P1b, p1a, p1b, p1a, p1b, p1a, p1b, p1a. (54 sts.)

6. (WS) *k1a, k1b*, repeat section in stars until end of row.

7. *P1b, p1a*, repeat section in stars until end of row.

8. Repeat steps 6 and 7 until your piece measures 4½in from the cast-on edge (5 more rows), ending with a WS row.

9. You will now start to increase for the thumb. *P1b, p1a*, repeat section in stars until you have 24 sts on the right needle. P1b, yb, CDI(aba), k1b, CDI(aba), yf, repeat section in stars until end of row. (58 sts.)

10. *K1a, k1b*, repeat section in stars until you have 26 sts on the right needle. Yf, p1a, p1b, p1a, p1b, p1a, yb, k1b. Repeat section in stars until end of row.

11. *K1b, k1a*, repeat section in stars until you have 24 sts on the right needle. K1b, CDI(aba), k1b, k1a, k1b, k1a, k1b, CDI(aba), repeat section in stars until end of row. (62 sts.)

12. *P1a, p1b*, repeat section in stars until end of row.

13. *K1b, k1a*, repeat section in stars until you have 24 sts on the right needle. K1b, CDI(aba), k1b, k1a, k1b, k1a, k1b, k1a, k1b, k1a, k1b, CDI(aba), repeat section in stars until end of row. (66 sts.)

14. Repeat step 12 once more.

15. *K1b, k1a*, repeat section in stars until you have 24 sts on the right needle. K1b, CDI(aba), k1b, k1a, k1b, k1a, k1b, k1a, k1b, k1a, k1b, k1a, k1b, k1a, k1b, CDI(aba). Repeat section in stars until end of row. (70 sts.)

16. Repeat step 12 once more.

17. *K1b, k1a*, repeat section in stars until you have 24 sts on the right needle. K1b, CDI(aba), k1b, k1a, k1b, k1a, k1b, k1a, k1b, k1a, k1b, k1a, k1b, k1a, k1b, k1a, k1b, CDI(aba). Repeat section in stars until end of row. (74 sts.)

18. Repeat step 12 once more.

19. *K1b, k1a*, repeat section in stars until you have 26 sts on the right needle. M1a, repeat section in stars until 28 sts remain, k1b, turn your work. You will now work back on these sts.

20. *P1b, p1a*, repeat section in stars until 26 sts remain, turn your work. You will now be working over these 22 sts only to make the thumb. (22 sts.)

21. *K1a, k1b*, repeat section in stars working 22 sts, turn your work.

22. *P1b, p1a*, repeat section in stars working 22 sts, turn your work.

23. Repeat steps 21 and 22 a further 4 times (8 more rows).

24. K1a, *sskb, k2toga*, repeat section in stars until 1 st remains, k1b. (12 sts.)

25. Cut yarn leaving a 6in tail. Thread a tapestry needle with the yarn tail and insert it through each of the 12 sts, starting with the furthest away. Remove knitting needle and pull yarn to close top of thumb. Use the vertical invisible seam technique to join the thumb seam down to the base of the thumb.

26. RS facing you, re-join yarn to the sts on the right needle. With color B pick up and k1 at base of thumb. Knit sts from the left needle as follows: k1a, *k1b, k1a*, repeat section in stars until the end of the row. Turn your work; you will now work back across all 54 sts.

27. *P1a, p1b*, repeat section in stars until end of row.

28. *P1b, p1a*, repeat section in stars until end of row.

29. Repeat steps 6 and 7 until the zig-zag section measures 1½in (9 more rows), ending with a WS row.

30. *K1b, k1a*, repeat section in stars until end of row.

31. Repeat steps 2 and 3 until vertical stripe section measures 1½in (9 more rows), ending with a WS row.

32. *P1b, p1a*, repeat section in stars until end of row.

33. *K1a, k1b*, repeat section in stars until end of row.

34. P2togb, p1b, *p1a, p1b*, repeat section in stars until you have 24 sts on the right needle, CDDPa, p1b. Repeat section in stars until 3 sts remain, p1a, p2togtbla. (50 sts.)

35. K1a, *k1a, k1b*, repeat section in stars until 1 st remains, k1b.

36. P2togb, p1a, *p1b, p1a*, repeat section in stars until you have 22 sts on the right needle, CDDPb, p1a. Repeat section in stars until 3 sts remain, p1b, p2togtbla. (46 sts.)

37. *K1a, k1b* repeat section in stars until end of row.

38. P2togb, p1b, *p1a, p1b*, repeat section in stars until you have 20 sts on the right needle, CDDPa, p1b. Repeat section in stars until 3 sts remain, p1a, p2togtbla. (42 sts.)

39. Sska, *k1b, k1a*, repeat section in stars until you have 19 sts on the right needle, CDDb, k1a. Repeat section in stars until 2 sts remain, k2togb. (38 sts.)

40. P2togb, p1b, *p1a, p1b*, repeat section in stars until you have 16 sts on the right needle, CDDPa, p1b. Repeat section in stars until 3 sts remain, p1a, p2togtbla. (34 sts.)

41. Sska, *k1b, k1a*, repeat section in stars until you have 15 sts on the right needle, CDDb, k1a. Repeat section in stars until 2 sts remain, k2togb. (30 sts.)

42. Cut yarn leaving a 6in tail. Thread a tapestry needle with the yarn tail and insert it through each of the sts on your needle, starting with the furthest away. Remove knitting needle and pull yarn to close top of mitten. Weave in any loose ends.

43. RS facing outwards, join the side seam using the vertical invisible seam technique and one strand of yarn. For the zig-zag sections, see it as 10 rows of twisted A and B floats. Insert needle through a row of floats on one side, then through the opposite row of floats on the other side. Pull yarn through and continue joining in this way.

We recommend you block your mittens to even out the stitches and achieve the correct measurements.

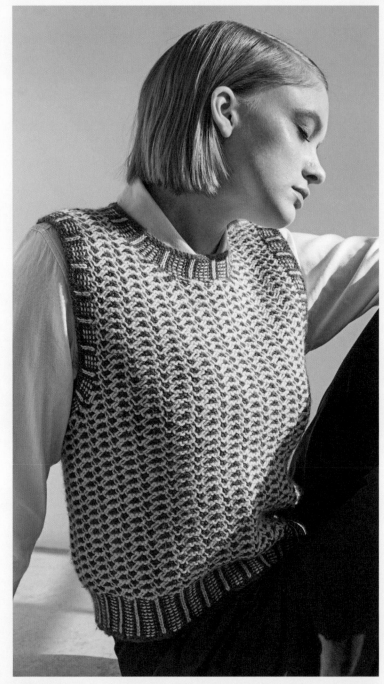

Looped stripe stitch

Knit

Wave vest

Combining garter rib stitch for the trims and looped stripe stitch for the body, the Wave vest makes for a versatile layering piece all year round. It is knitted in the round from the bottom up to the armholes, where the stitches are split in half, working the front and back separately flat. The shoulder seams are joined, and then stitches are picked up around the neck and armholes to work the trims in the round.

Size
This pattern includes 8 sizes. See page 150 for size chart. Iris wears size 2.

Flat measurements

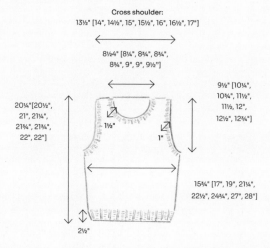

Cross shoulder:
13½" [14", 14½", 15", 15½", 16", 16½", 17"]

8½4" [8¼", 8¾", 8¾", 8¾", 9", 9", 9½"]

9½" [10¼", 10¾", 11½", 11½", 12", 12½", 12¾"]

20¼"[20½", 21", 21¼", 21¾", 21¾", 22", 22"]

1½"

1"

15¾" [17", 19", 21¼", 22½", 24¾", 27", 28"]

2½"

Yarn
DK weight yarn in 2 colors.
You will need approx. 343yds/314m [405yds/370m, 453yds/414m, 514yds/470m, 551yds/504m, 612yds/560m, 674yds/616m, 735yds/672m] of color A and 313yds/286m [373yd/341m, 421yds/385m, 481yds/440m, 517yds/473m, 577yds/528m, 638yds/583m, 698yds/638m] of color B.

We used
Color A – Blue
3 [4, 4, 5, 5, 5, 6, 6] balls of UK Alpaca Superfine Alpaca DK in Midnight Blue – 75% superfine alpaca, 25% wool (123yds/112m per 50g ball)

Color B – White
2 [2, 2, 2, 3, 3, 3, 3] balls of By Laxtons Sheepsoft DK in Airedale – 100% British wool (241yds/220m per 100g ball)

In the Pink-and-white sample, we used UK Alpaca Superfine Alpaca DK in Rose and Stylecraft Naturals Organic Cotton DK in Bone

Alternative yarn suggestions: Sandnes Garn Double Sunday, Drops Karisma, Lang Yarns Merino 120

Recommended needles
US 7 (4.5mm) circular knitting needles, length: 32–40in and 20in.
US 8 (5mm) circular knitting needles, length: 32–40in.

Gauge
Garter rib stitch (see page 31) after blocking on US 7 (4.5mm) needles: 4 x 4in = 22.5 stitches x 43 rows
Looped stripe stitch (see page 28) after blocking on US 8 (5mm) needles: 4 x 4in= 21 stitches x 38 rows

Knitting notes
Please refer to the charts on pages 160–3 when referenced in the instructions.

Instructions

Body

1. With US 7 (4.5mm) circular needles, length 32–40in and color A, cast on 168 [180, 204, 228, 240, 264, 288, 300] sts using the long tail cast on technique.

   Place a st marker and join to work in the round, being careful not to twist your sts.

2. *K3, p3*, repeat section in stars (*) until end of round.

3. With color B, *sl1pwyib, k1, sl1pwyib, p3*, repeat section in stars until end of round.

4. Repeat rounds 1 and 2 of garter rib st worked in the round (see page 31), until your piece measures 2½in from the cast-on edge (approx. a further 24 rounds), ending with a round 2, color B row.

5. With US 8 (5mm) circular needles, length 32–40in and color B, k all sts.

6. With color B, p all sts.

7. Repeat rounds 1 to 4 of looped stripe st worked in the round (see page 28), until your piece measures 10¾in [10½in, 10½in, 10in, 10in, 9¾in, 9¾in, 9¼in] from the cast-on edge (approx. 20 [19, 19, 18, 18, 17, 17, 16] repeats in total, 80 [76, 76, 72, 72, 68, 68, 64] rounds). Make sure last round worked is round 4.

8. With color A, bind off 4 sts, k80 [86, 98, 110, 116, 128, 140, 146]. Turn your work.

You will now be working back and forth over these 80 [86, 98, 110, 116, 128, 140, 146] sts to make the back of your vest. (You will come back to the other sts later.)

9. Bind off 4 sts, k76 [82, 94, 106, 112, 124, 136, 144]. Turn your work. (76 [82, 94, 106, 112, 124, 136, 142] sts.)

10. With color B, ssk, *k1, loop1L, k3, loop1R*, repeat section in stars until 2 sts remain, k2tog. (74 [80, 92, 104, 110, 122, 134, 140] sts.)

11. K all sts.

12. With color A, ssk, k until 2 sts remain, k2tog. (72 [78, 90, 102, 108, 120, 132, 138] sts.)

13. K all sts.

14. With color B, ssk, k3, loop1R, *k1, loop1L, k3, loop1R*, repeat section in stars until 6 sts remain, k1, loop1L, k2, k2tog. (70 [76, 88, 100, 106, 118, 130, 136] sts.)

15. Repeat steps 11 to 13 once more. (68 [74, 86, 98, 104, 116, 128, 134] sts.)

16. With color B, ssk, k1, loop1R, *k1, loop1L, k3, loop1R*, repeat section in stars until 4 sts remain, k1, loop1L, k2tog. (66 [72, 84, 96, 102, 114, 126, 132] sts.)

17. Repeat steps 11 to 13 once more. (64 [70, 82, 94, 100, 112, 124, 130] sts.)

   Sizes 2, 3, 4, 5, 6, 7 and 8 only:
18. Repeat steps 10 to [13, 17, 17, 17, 17, 17, 17] a further [1, 1, 1, 2, 3, 3, 4] times. ([66, 70, 82, 76, 76, 88, 82] sts.)

Sizes 3, 4, 5 and 7 only:

19. Repeat steps 10 to [11, 16, 11, 15] once more. ([68, 72, 74, 80] sts.)

Sizes 1, 2, 4, 6, 7 and 8 only:

20. Work row(s) 3–4 [3–4, 4, 3–4, 3–4, 3–4] of the repeat chart [looped stripe st worked flat, repeat chart, repeat chart, repeat chart, repeat chart].

All sizes:

21. Repeat rows 1 to 4 of the repeat chart [looped stripe st worked flat, repeat chart, repeat chart, repeat chart, repeat chart, repeat chart, repeat chart] until your piece measures 19½in [20in, 20¼in, 20½in, 20¾in, 20¾in, 21¼in, 21¼in] from the cast-on edge (approx. 16 [17, 16, 15, 15, 13, 12, 12] full repeats and 3 rows, 67 [71, 67, 63, 63, 55, 51, 51] rows in total. Make sure last row worked is row 3.

22. (WS) With color B, k14 [15, 15, 17, 18, 18, 20, 20] sts. Turn your work.

    You will now work over these 14 [15, 15, 17, 18, 18, 20, 20] sts only to form one side of your back neck. (You will come back to the other sts later.)

23. Work rows 1 to 8 of the left back neck chart. Make sure you follow the correct chart for your size.

24. Bind off 11 [12, 12, 14, 15, 15, 17, 17] sts.

25. Go back to the 50 [51, 53, 55, 56, 58, 60, 62] sts you left in step 22. WS facing you, working from left to right, slip the next 36 [36, 38, 38, 38, 40, 40, 42] sts onto a st

holder or scrap piece of yarn. (You will come back to these sts when knitting your neck trim.)

26. WS facing you, re-join color B to the 14 [15, 15, 17, 18, 18, 20, 20] sts waiting on your needle. K14 [15, 15, 15, 18, 18, 20, 20] sts.

27. Work rows 1 to 8 of the right back neck chart.

28. Bind off 11 [12, 12, 14, 15, 15, 17, 17] sts.

    Now the back of your vest is complete, it's time to work the front.

29. RS facing you, re-join color A to the 84 [90, 102, 114, 120, 132, 144, 150] sts waiting on your needle from step 8. Bind off 4 sts, k until end of row. (80 [86, 98, 110, 116, 128, 140, 146] sts.)

30. Bind off 4 sts, k until end of row. (76 [82, 94, 106, 112, 124, 136, 142] sts.)

31. Repeat steps 10 to 20 once more. Follow only the steps for your size. (64 [66, 68, 72, 74, 76, 80, 82] sts.)

32. Repeat rows 1 to 4 of the repeat chart [looped stripe st worked flat, repeat chart, repeat chart, repeat chart, repeat chart, repeat chart, repeat chart] until your piece measures 16in [16¼in, 16½in, 16¼in, 16¾in, 16¼in, 16¾in, 16¼in] from the cast-on edge (approx. 8 [8, 7, 5, 5, 2, 1, 0] full repeats and 3 rows, 35 [35, 31, 23, 23, 11, 7, 3] rows in total). Make sure last row worked is row 3.

33. (WS) With color B, k25 [26, 26, 28, 29, 29, 31, 31] sts. Turn your work. You will now work over these 25 [26, 26, 28, 29, 29, 31, 31] sts only to form one side of your front neck. (You will come back to the other sts later.)

34. Work rows 1 to 28 [24, 28, 28, 28, 28, 28, 28] of the left front neck chart.

35. Repeat rows 25 [1, 25, 25, 25, 25, 25, 25] to 28 [4, 28, 28, 28, 28, 28, 28] of the left front neck chart [looped stripe st worked flat, left front neck chart, left front neck chart, left front neck chart, left front neck chart, left front neck chart, left front neck chart] until your piece measures 20¼in [20½in, 21in, 21¼in, 21¾in, 21¾in, 22in, 22in] from the cast-on edge (approx. 3 [5, 4, 5, 5, 6, 6, 7] repeats, 12 [20, 16, 20, 20, 24, 24, 28] rows in total). Make sure last row worked is row 4.

36. Bind off 11 [12, 12, 14, 15, 15, 17, 17] sts.

37. Go back to the 39 [40, 42, 44, 45, 47, 49, 51] sts you left in step 33. WS facing you, working from left to right, slip the next 14 [14, 16, 16, 16, 18, 18, 20] sts onto a st holder or scrap piece of yarn. (You will come back to these when knitting the neck.)

38. WS facing you, rejoin color B to the 25 [26, 26, 28, 29, 29, 31, 31] sts waiting on your needle. K25 [26, 26, 28, 29, 29, 31, 31] sts.

39. Work rows 1 to 28 [24, 28, 28, 28, 28, 28, 28] of the right front neck chart.

40. Repeat rows 25 [1, 25, 25, 25, 25, 25, 25] to 28 [4, 28, 28, 28, 28, 28, 28] of the right front neck chart [looped stripe st worked flat, right front neck chart, right front neck chart, right front neck chart, right front neck chart, right front neck chart, right front neck chart] until your piece measures 20¼in [20½in, 21in, 21¼in, 21¾in, 21¾in, 22in, 22in] from the cast-on edge (approx. 3 [5, 4, 5, 5, 6, 6, 7] repeats, 12 [20, 16, 20, 20, 24, 24, 28] rows in total). Make sure last row worked is row 4.

41. Bind off 11 [12, 12, 14, 15, 15, 17, 17] sts.

Shoulder seams

RS of vest facing outwards, use the horizontal invisible seam technique to sew the front and back shoulder seams together.

Neck trim

1. With US 7 (4.5mm) circular needles, length 20in and color A, pick up and knit sts around the neckline as follows:

Working from right to left, start at front right shoulder seam. Pick up 21 [21, 22, 22, 22, 23, 23, 24] sts from shoulder seam along the front right neckline until you reach sts on st holder. K14 [14, 16, 16, 16, 18, 18, 20] sts from st holder, then pick up 21 [21, 22, 22, 22, 23, 23, 24] sts along the left front until you reach the left shoulder seam. Now pick up 2 sts around back neck until you reach sts on st holder. K36 [36, 38, 38, 38, 40, 40, 42] sts from st holder, then pick up 2 sts around back neck until you reach the point where you started. (96 [96, 102, 102, 102, 108, 108, 114] sts.)

Place st marker and join to work in the round.

2. With color B, *sl1pwyib, k1, sl1pwyib, p3*, repeat section in stars until end of round.

3. Repeat rounds 1 and 2 of garter rib st worked in the round until your trim measures 1¼in (approx. 11 rounds). Make sure last round worked is round 1, color A row.

4. With color A, *k3, p3*, repeat section in stars until end of round.

5. With color A, bind off in ribbing.

Armhole trims

Repeat instructions twice to knit the left and right trims.

1. Using US 7 (4.5mm) circular needles, length 20in and color A, pick up and knit 108 [114, 120, 126, 132, 138, 138, 144] sts in total around the armhole as follows:

   RS facing outwards, start at the centre of the underarm bind off. Working from right to left, pick up 54 [57, 60 ,63, 66, 69, 69, 72] sts from the underarm to shoulder seam, then 54 [57, 60, 63, 66, 69, 69, 72] sts from shoulder seam to the centre of the underarm bind off.

2. Place st marker and join to work in the round.

   With color B, *sl1pwyib, k1, sl1pwyib, p3*, repeat section in stars until end of round.

3. Repeat rounds 1 and 2 of garter rib st worked in the round, until your trim measures ¾in (approx. 7 rounds). Make sure last round worked is round 1, color A row.

4. With color A, *k3, p3*, repeat section in stars until end of round.

5. With color A, bind off in ribbing tightly.

Weave in all loose ends. We recommend you block your vest to even out the fabric and achieve the correct measurements.

The Wave vest celebrates the Hokusai print, 'The Great Wave'.

The wrap around

Essentially a scarf with sleeves, The wrap around can be worn as a scarf or as sleeves. Knitted in all-over stockinette stitch, the sleeves are worked in the round with rib cuffs while the central section is worked flat in stockinette stitch, with ribbed edging.

Size

The pattern includes 4 sizes; if you are a size 1-2 follow the first size, size 3-4 follow the second size, size 5-6 follow the third size and size 7-8 follow the fourth size. When the instructions differ between sizes, they will be written as follows: size 1-2 [size 3-4, size 5-6, size 7-8]. See page 150 for size chart. Lydia wears size 1-2.

Flat measurements

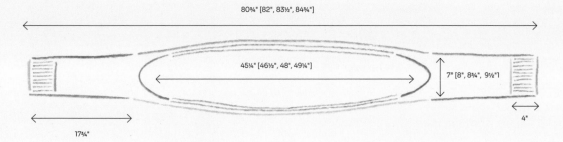

80¾" [82", 83½", 84¾"]

45¼" [46½", 48", 49¼"]

7" [8", 8¾", 9½"]

17¾"

4"

Yarn

Worsted weight yarn held double, or bulky weight yarn with approx. 77yds/70m per 50g. We recommend using a lightweight alpaca blend yarn so that it's soft against the skin and not too heavy on the neck.

We used the yarn from page 18 but here are some similar suggestions:

Worsted weight yarn held double

6 [7, 8, 9] balls of Lana Grossa Brigitte no. 2 in color 09 – 47% alpaca, 45% cotton, 8% wool (153yds/140m per 50g ball)
Alternative yarn suggestions: CaMaRose Snefnug, Drops Air, Wool and the Gang Feeling Good yarn

Chunky

7 [8, 9, 10] balls of Lana Grossa Ecopuno Chunky in color 118 – 48% cotton, 33% Merino wool, 9% alpaca (77yds/70m per 50g ball)
Alternative yarn suggestion: Drops Wish

Stockinette stitch

Recommended needles

US 10.5 (7mm) circular knitting needles,
    length 16–20in
US 15 (10mm) circular knitting needles,
    length 16–20in

Gauge

Stockinette stitch after blocking on US 15 (10mm)
needles: 4 x 4in = 10 stitches x 12 rows

Instructions

1. With US 10.5 (7mm) needles, cast on 36 [40, 44, 48] sts using the long tail cast on technique.

   Place st marker and join to work in the round, being careful not to twist your sts.

2. *K2, p2*, repeat section in stars (*) until end of round.

3. Repeat step 2 until your piece measures 4in from the cast-on edge (approx. a further 15 rounds).

4. With US 15 (10mm) needles, k all sts.

5. Repeat step 4 until your piece measures 17¾in from the cast on edge (approx. 42 rounds).

   The first sleeve is now complete. You will now work the section that wraps around the neck. This section is worked flat, so you need to turn your work after every row. Remove st marker and turn your work.

6. (WS) sl1p, k1, p1, k1, purl until 4 sts remain, k1, p1, k1, p1. Turn your work.

7. (RS) sl1k, p1, k1, p1, k until 4 sts remain, p1, k1, p1, k1. Turn your work.

8. Repeat steps 6 and 7 until your piece measures 45¼in [46½in, 48in, 49¼in] from the end of the first sleeve (approx. a further 136 [140, 144, 148] rows). Make sure last row worked is a RS row.

The wrap section is now finished. You will now go back to working in the round to make the second sleeve. RS facing outwards, place a marker and join to work in the round.

9. Repeat step 4 until your sleeve measures 13¾in (approx. 42 rounds).

10. With US 10.5 (7mm) needles, repeat step 2 until your rib measures 4in (approx. a further 16 rounds).

11. Bind off loosely in ribbing.

12. Weave in all loose ends.

Depending on which yarn you are using, you may want to block your scarf to achieve the correct measurements.

To wear: Insert one arm through one sleeve, then wrap the middle section around the neck as follows: around the back of the neck, across the front of the neck and around the back again. You are now in position to insert the other arm in the second sleeve. Voila!

Patterns

Pillar and web stitch

Knit

Scribble top

The Scribble top has a simple, slightly loose-fitting shape and is knitted from the bottom up in an open pillar and web stitch. The top is knitted flat in two pieces, the front and the back. Decreases are made to shape the armhole and neckline, while slip stitches keep the edges neat. The shoulder and side seams are joined using invisible seams.

Size
This pattern includes 8 sizes; see page 150 for size chart. Sana wears size 2.

Flat measurements

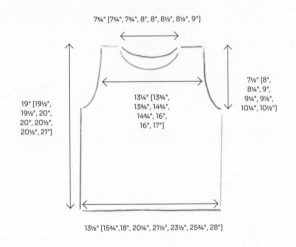

7¾" [7¾", 7¾", 8", 8", 8½", 8½", 9"]

7½" [8", 8¼", 9", 9¼", 9½", 10¼", 10½"]

19" [19½", 19½", 20", 20", 20½", 20½", 21"]

13¼" [13¾", 13¾", 14¾", 14¾", 16", 16", 17"]

13½" [15¾",18", 20¼", 21½", 23½", 25¾", 28"]

Yarn
Fingering weight yarn, approx. 168yds/155m per 50g. You will need approx. 457yds /418m [525yds/480m, 610yds/558m, 712yds/651m, 746yds/682m, 820yds/750m, 899yds/822m, 1017yds/930m].

We used
3 [4, 4, 5, 5, 5, 6, 6] balls of Quince & Co Sparrow in Eclipse – 100% organic linen (168yds/155m per 50g ball)

Alternative yarn suggestions: Lang Yarns Crealino, BC Garn Lino

Recommended needles
US 8 (5mm) knitting needles
US 15 (10mm) knitting needles

Gauge
Pillar and web stitch (see page 32) after blocking:
4 x 4in = 21 stitches x 17 rows

Knitting notes
- To get the neatest edge for seaming and the armhole and neckline, make sure that the edge stitches are pulled really tight before you start a new row.

- When casting off stitches at the neckline, be aware of your gauge. Do not bind off too tightly or the neckline will be too small.

- When decreasing in the pattern you will be asked to work variations of the sk3, p3 over, p3 technique on page 33—for example, 'sk2, p3 over, p2' or 'sk2, p2 over, p2' or 'sk3, p3 over, p2tog, p1'. Please note this is the same technique—you just change the number of stitches you skip or purl over.

Instructions

Back

1. With US 8 (5mm) needles, cast on 74 [86, 98, 110, 116, 128, 140, 152] sts using the cable cast on technique.

2. (RS) Using a US 15 (10mm) needle, k all sts.

   From this point onwards, you will alternate between US 15 (10mm) and US 8 (5mm) needles every row. If you are using interchangeable needles, you can adjust your needles at this point to one US 15 (10mm) and one US 8 (5mm) needle.

3. (WS) Using a US 8 (5mm) needle, p1, *sk3, p3 over, p3*, repeat section in (*) stars until 1 st remains, p1.

4. Repeat steps 2 and 3 until your piece measures 11½in [11½in, 11¼in, 11¼in, 10¾in, 10¾in, 10¼in, 10¼in] from the cast-on edge (approx. 48 [48, 46, 46, 44, 44, 42, 42] more rows). Make sure last row is a WS row.

   You will now start decreasing for the armhole. To help when seaming, place a stitch marker or scrap piece of yarn at each end of the work to mark the underarm.

Sizes 5, 6, 7 and 8 only:

5. Using a US 8 (5mm) needle, bind off [6, 6, 12, 12] sts. Slip the st on the right needle back onto the left, then using a US 15 (10mm) needle sl1pwyib, k all sts. ([110, 122, 128, 140] sts.)

6. Using a US 8 (5mm) needle, bind off [6, 6, 12, 12] sts. Slip the st on the right needle back

onto the left, sl1p, *sk3, p3 over, p3*, repeat section in stars until 1 st remains, p1. ([104, 116, 116, 128] sts.)

All sizes:

7. Using a US 15 (10mm) needle, sl1pwyib, k9, ssk, k until 9 sts remain, k2tog, k7. (72 [84, 96, 108, 102, 114, 114, 126] sts.) For size 1, skip to step 23.

Sizes 2, 3, 4, 5, 6, 7 and 8 only:

8. Using a US 8 (5mm) needle, sl1p, *sk3, p3 over, p3*, sk2, p3 over, p2tog. Repeat section in stars until 12 sts remain, sk2, p3 over, p2togtbl, sk3, p3over, p4. ([82, 94, 106, 100, 112, 112, 124] sts.)

9. Using a US 15 (10mm) needle, sl1pwyib, k until end of row.

10. Using a US 8 (5mm) needle, sl1p, *sk3, p3 over, p3*, sk2, p2 over, p2tog. Repeat section in stars until 11 sts remain, sk2, p2 over, p2togtbl, sk3, p3over, p4. ([80, 92, 104, 98, 110, 110, 122] sts.)

11. Using a US 15 (10mm) needle, sl1pwyib, k until end of row.

12. Using a US 8 (5mm) needle/, sl1p, *sk3, p3 over, p3*, sk2, p1 over, p2tog. Repeat section in stars until 10 sts remain, sk2, p1 over, p2togtbl, sk3, p3over, p4. ([78, 90, 102, 96, 108, 108, 120] sts.)

13. Using a US 15 (10mm) needle, sl1pwyib, k until end of row.

14. Using a US 8 (5mm) needle, sl1p, *sk3, p3 over, p3*, p2tog. Repeat section in stars until 9 sts remain, p2togtbl, sk3, p3 over, p4. ([76, 88, 100, 94, 106, 106, 118] sts.)

15. Using a US 15 (10mm) needle, sl1pwyib, k until end of row.

16. Using a US 8 (5mm) needle, sl1p, sk4, p3 over, p2tog, p2, *sk3, p3 over, p3*. Repeat section in stars until 8 sts remain, sk4, p3 over, p2togtbl, p3. ([74, 86, 98, 92, 104, 104, 116 sts.)

Sizes 3, 4, 5, 6, 7 and 8 only:
17. Repeat steps 7 to 16 a further [1, 1, 1, 1, 1, 2] times. ([74, 86, 80, 92, 92, 92] sts.)

Sizes 4, 6 and 7 only:
18. Repeat steps 7 to 9 once more. ([82, 88, 88] sts.)

19. Using a US 8 (5mm) needle, sl1p, sk3, p3 over, p2tog, p1, sk1, p3 over, p1, *sk3, p3 over, p3*. Repeat section in stars until 11 sts remain, sk1, p3 over, p1, sk3, p3 over, p2togtbl, p2. ([80, 86, 86] sts.)

20. Using a US 15 (10mm) needle, sl1pwyib, k until end of row.

21. Using a US 8 (5mm) needle, sl1p, sk2, p3 over, p2, sk1, p3 over, p1, *sk3, p3 over, p3*. Repeat section in stars until 10 sts remain, sk1, p3 over, p1, sk2, p3 over, p3.

22. Repeat steps 20 and 21 until your piece measures [20in, 20½in, 20½in] from the cast-on edge (approx. [12, 14, 16] more rows). Make sure last row is a WS row.

Size 1 only:
23. (WS) Using a US 8 (5mm) needle, sl1p, *sk3, p3 over, p3*, sk2, p3 over, p2. Repeat section in stars until 12 sts remain, sk2, p3 over, p2, sk3, p3 over, p4.

24. Using a US 15 (10mm) needle, sl1pwyib, k until end of row.

25. Repeat steps 23 and 24 until your piece measures 19in from the cast-on edge (approx. 29 more rows). Make sure last row is a WS row.

Sizes 2, 3, 5 and 8 only:
26. Using a US 15 (10mm) needle, sl1pwyib, k until end of row.

27. Using a US 8 (5mm) needle, sl1p, *sk3, p3 over, p3*, repeat section in stars until 1 st remains, p1.

28. Repeat steps 26 and 27 until your piece measures [19½in, 19½in,20in, 21in] from the cast-on edge (approx [22, 14, 16, 12] more rows). Make sure last row is a WS row.

All sizes:
29. Using a US 8 (5mm) needle, bind off.

Front

1. Repeat steps 1 to 19 as for the back, following only the steps for your size. (72 [74, 74, 80, 80, 86, 86, 92] sts.)

Size 1 only:

2. Repeat steps 23 and 24 of the back until your piece measures 18in from the cast-on edge (approx. 27 more rows). Make sure last row is a WS row.

Sizes 2, 3, 5 and 8 only:

3. Repeat steps 26 and 27 of the back until your piece measures [18in, 18½in, 18¾in, 18½in] from the cast-on edge (approx. [20, 12, 12, 4] more rows). Make sure last row is a WS row.

Sizes 4, 6 and 7 only:

4. Repeat steps 20 and 21 of the back until your piece measures 18¾in from the cast-on edge (approx. [8, 8, 10] more rows). Make sure last row is a WS row.

Sizes 1, 2 and 3 only:

5. Using a US 15 (10mm) needle, sl1pwyib, k17 [18, 18]. Turn your work.

You will now be working over these 18 [19, 19] sts only to make one side of your front neck. (You will come back to the other sts later.)

6. Using a US 8 (5mm) needle, sl1p, sk2, p3 over, p2, sk2 [3, 3], p3 over, p2tog, p0[1, 1], sk3, p3 over, p4. (17 [18, 18] sts.)

7. Using a US 15 (10mm) needle, sl1pwyib, k16 [17, 17].

8. Using a US 8 (5mm) needle, sl1p, sk2, p3 over, p2, sk2, p2 [3, 3] over, p2tog, sk3, p3 over, p4. (16 [17, 17] sts.)

9. Using a US 8 (5mm) needle, bind off 16 [17, 17] sts.

10. RS facing outwards, re-join yarn to 54 [55, 55] sts waiting on your needle. Using a US 8 (5mm) needle, bind off 36 sts. Slip the st on the right needle onto the left. (18 [19, 19] sts.)

11. Using a US 15 (10mm) needle, sl1pwyib, k until end of row.

12. Using a US 8 (5mm) needle, sl1p, sk3, p3 over, p3, sk2 [3, 3], p3 over, p0[1, 1], p2togtbl, sk2, p3 over, p3. (17 [18, 18] sts.)

13. Using a US 15 (10mm) needle, sl1pwyib, k until end of row.

14. Using a US 8 (5mm) needle, sl1p, sk3, p3 over, p3, sk2, p2 [3, 3] over, p2togtbl, sk2, p3 over, p3. (16 [17, 17] sts.)

15. Using a US 8 (5mm) needle, bind off.

16. **Size 4 only:**
Using a US 15 (10mm) needle, sl1pwyib, k21. Turn your work.

You will now be working over these 22 sts only to make one side of your front neck. (You will come back to the other sts later.)

17. Using a US 8 (5mm) needle, sl1p, sk2, p3 over, p2tog, sk3, p3 over, p3, sk1, p3 over, p1, sk2, p3 over, p3. (21 sts.)

18. Using a US 15 (10mm) needle, sl1pwyib, k20.

19. Using a US 8 (5mm) needle, sl1p, sk1, p3 over, p1, sk3, p3 over, p2tog, p1, sk1, p3 over, p1, sk2, p3 over, p3. (20 sts.)

20. Using a US 15 (10mm) needle, sl1pwyib, k19.

21. Using a US 8 (5mm) needle, sl1p, sk1, p3 over, p1, sk2, p3 over, p2tog, sk1, p3 over, p1, sk2, p3 over, p3. (19 sts.)

22. Using a US 8 (5mm) needle, bind off 19 sts.

23. RS facing outwards, re-join yarn to 58 sts waiting on your needle. Using a US 8 (5mm) needle, bind off 36 sts. Slip the st on the right needle onto the left. (22 sts.)

24. Using a US 15 (10mm) needle, sl1pwyib, k until end of row.

25. Using a US 8 (5mm) needle, sl1p, sk2, p3 over, p2, sk1, p3 over, p1, sk3, p3 over, p3, sk2, p3 over, p2togtbl, p1. (21 sts.)

26. Using a US 15 (10mm) needle, sl1pwyib, k until end of row.

27. Using a US 8 (5mm) needle, sl1p, sk2, p3 over, p2, sk1, p3 over, p1, sk3, p3 over, p1, p2togtbl, sk1, p3 over, p2. (20 sts.)

28. Using a US 15 (10mm) needle, sl1pwyib, k until end of row.

29. Using a US 8 (5mm) needle, sl1p, sk2, p3 over, p2, sk1, p3 over, p1, sk2, p3 over, p2togtbl, sk1, p3 over, p2. (19 sts.)

30. Using a US 8 (5mm) needle, bind off.

Size 5 only:
31. Using a US 15 (10mm) needle, sl1pwyib, k20. Turn your work.

You will now be working over these 21 sts only to make one side of your front neck. (You will come back to the other sts later.)

32. Using a US 8 (5mm) needle, sl1p, sk4, p3 over, p2tog, p2, sk3, p3 over, p3, sk3, p3 over, p4. (20 sts.)

33. Using a US 15 (10mm) needle, sl1pwyib, k19.

34. Using a US 8 (5mm) needle, sl1p, sk3, p3 over, p3, sk3, p3 over, p2tog, p1, sk3, p3 over, p4. (19 sts.)

35. Using a US 15 (10mm) needle, sl1pwyib, k18.

36. Using a US 8 (5mm) needle, sl1p, sk3, p3 over, p3, sk2, p3 over, p2, sk3, p3 over, p4.

37. Using a US 8 (5mm) needle, bind off 19 sts.

38. RS facing outwards, re-join yarn to 59 sts waiting on your needle. Using a US 8 (5mm) needle, bind off 38 sts. Slip the st on the right needle onto the left. (21 sts.)

39. Using a US 15 (10mm) needle, sl1pwyib, k until end of row.

40. Using a US 8 (5mm) needle, sl1p, sk3, p3 over, p3, sk3, p3 over, p3, sk4, p3 over, p2togtbl, p3. (20 sts.)

41. Using a US 15 (10mm) needle, sl1pwyib, k until end of row.

42. Using a US 8 (5mm) needle, sl1p, sk3, p3 over, p3, sk3, p3 over, p1, p2togtbl, sk3, p3over, p4. (19 sts.)

43. Using a US 15 (10mm) needle, sl1pwyib, k until end of row.

44. Using a US 8 (5mm) needle, sl1p, sk3, p3 over, p3, sk2, p3 over, p2, sk3, p3 over, p4.

45. Using a US 8 (5mm) needle, bind off.

Sizes 6, 7 and 8 only:

46. Using a US 15 (10mm) needle, sl1pwyib, k[23, 23, 26]. Turn your work.

    You will now be working over these [24, 24, 27] sts only to make one side of your front neck. (You will come back to the other sts later.)

47. Using a US 8 (5mm) needle, sl1p, sk4, p3 over, p2tog, p2, sk3, p3 over, p3, sk[1, 1, 3], p3 over, p[1, 1, 3] sk[2, 2, 3], p3 over, p[3, 3, 4]. ([23, 23, 26] sts.)

48. Using a US 15 (10mm) needle, sl1pwyib, k[22, 22, 25].

49. Using a US 8 (5mm) needle, sl1p, sk3, p3 over, p2tog, p1, sk3, p3 over, p3, sk[1, 1, 3], p3 over, p[1, 1, 3], sk[2, 2, 3], p3 over, p[3, 3, 4]. ([22, 22, 25] sts.)

50. Using a US 15 (10mm) needle, sl1pwyib, k[21, 21, 24].

51. Using a US 8 (5mm) needle, sl1p, sk2, p3 over, p2tog, sk3, p3 over, p3, sk[1, 1, 3], p3 over, p[1, 1, 3], sk[2, 2, 3], p3 over, p[3, 3, 4]. ([21, 21, 24] sts.)

52. Using a US 15 (10mm) needle, sl1pwyib, k[20, 20, 23].

Sizes 6 and 7 only:

53. Using a US 8 (5mm) needle, sl1p, sk1, p3 over, p1, sk3, p3 over, p3, sk1, p3 over, p1, sk2, p3 over, p3.

54. Using a US 8 (5mm) needle, bind off 21 sts.

Size 8 only:

55. Using a US 8 (5mm) needle, sl1p, sk1, p3 over, p1, sk3, p3 over, p2tog, p1, sk3, p3 over, p3, sk3, p3 over, p4. (23 sts.)

56. Using a US 15 (10mm) needle, sl1pwyib, k22.

57. Using a US 8 (5mm) needle, sl1p, sk1, p3 over, p1, sk2, p3 over, p2, sk3, p3 over, p3, sk3, p3 over, p4.

58. Using a US 8 (5mm) needle, bind off 23 sts.

Sizes 6, 7 and 8 only:

59. RS facing outwards, re-join yarn to [62, 62, 65] sts waiting on your needle. Using a US 8 (5mm) needle, bind off 38 sts. Slip the st on the right needle onto the left. ([24, 24, 27 sts.)

60. Using a US 15 (10mm) needle, sl1pwyib, k until end of row.

61. Using a US 8 (5mm) needle, sl1p, sk[2, 2, 3], p3 over, p[2, 2, 3], sk[1, 1, 3], p3 over, p[1, 1, 3], sk3, p3 over, p3, sk4, p3 over, p2togtbl, p3. ([23, 23, 26] sts.)

62. Using a US 15 (10mm) needle, sl1pwyib, k until end of row.

63. Using a US 8 (5mm) needle, sl1p, sk[2, 2, 3], p3 over, p[2, 2, 3], sk[1, 1, 3], p3 over, p[1, 1, 3], sk3, p3 over, p3, sk3, p3 over, p2togtbl, p2. ([22, 22, 25] sts.)

64. Using a US 15 (10mm) needle, sl1pwyib, k until end of row.

65. Using a US 8 (5mm) needle, sl1p, sk[2, 2, 3], p3 over, p[2, 2, 3], sk[1, 1, 3], p3 over, p[1, 1, 3], sk3, p3 over, p3, sk2, p3 over, p2togtbl, p1. ([21, 21, 24] sts.)

66. Using a US 15 (10mm) needle, sl1pwyib, k until end of row.

Sizes 6 and 7 only:

67. Using a US 8 (5mm) needle, sl1p, sk2, p3 over, p2, sk1, p3 over, p1, sk3, p3 over, p3, sk1, p3 over, p2.

68. Using a US 8 (5mm) needle, bind off.

Size 8 only:

69. Using a US 8 (5mm) needle, sl1p, sk3, p3 over, p3, sk3, p3 over, p3, sk3, p3 over, p1, p2togtbl, sk1, p3 over, p2. (23 sts.)

70. Using a US 15 (10mm) needle, sl1pwyib, k until end of row.

71. Using a US 8 (5mm) needle, sl1p, sk3, p3 over, p3, sk3, p3 over, p3, sk2, p3 over, p2, sk1, p3 over, p2.

72. Using a US 8 (5mm) needle, bind off.

Shoulder seams

RS facing outwards, place the front on top of the back. Starting from the outside edges, use the horizontal invisible seam technique to sew the shoulder seams together.

Side seam

RS facing outwards, starting at the hem edge, use the vertical invisible seam technique to sew the sides of the front and back together. Stop when you reach the underarm markers placed in step 4.

Weave in all loose ends. We recommend blocking your top to even out the stitches and achieve the correct measurements.

Rush hood

Knitted using a two-color zig-zag jacquard stitch and 2 x 2 rib stitch, the Rush hood is knitted in one piece from the top down. First, a rectangle at the top of the hood is knitted, then stitches are picked up on either side to create the main section of the hood. These stitches are worked until you reach the bottom of the head, where the rib neck is knitted. Finally, stitches are picked up and knitted around the hood opening in rib.

Size
One size

Flat measurements

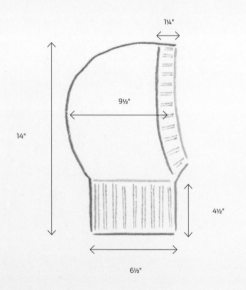

Yarn
Worsted weight yarn. You will need approx. 153yds/140m of color A and 77yds/70m of color B.

We used
Color A – Brown
    1 ball of De Rerum Natura, Gilliatt in Caramel – 100% Merino wool (273yds/250m per 100g ball)
Colour B – Light blue
    1 ball of Blue Sky Fibers, Woolstok in Thermal Spring – 100% fine Highland wool (123yds/112m per 50g ball)
In the Navy-and-blue sample, we used Kremke Soul Wool, The Merry Merino 70 in color 26 and 24. Alternative yarn suggestions: Fonty Tartan 6, Drops Alaska, Lana Grossa Bingo

Recommended needles
US 7 (4.5mm) circular knitting needles, length
    16–20in
US 10 (6mm) circular knitting needles, length
    16–20in

Gauge
Zig-zag jacquard stitch (see page 34) after blocking on US 10 (6mm) needles: 4 x 4in = 19 stitches x 42 rows

Zig-zag jacquard stitch

Instructions

1. With US 10 (6mm) needles and color A, cast on 18 sts using the cable cast on technique.

2. (RS) K all sts.

3. P all sts.

4. Work rows 1 to 12 of zig-zag jacquard st twice—see page 34 for st information. (24 rows.)

5. Repeat rows 1 to 10 of zig-zag jacquard st once more.

   You will now pick up sts on either side of this rectangle to create the main section of the hood. Cut the yarns leaving a 6in yarn tail and leave the sts on your needles.

6. RS facing outwards, needle at the top of the work. Start at the bottom right corner of the cast on. With the same needles and color A, pick up and k 32 sts until you reach the sts waiting on your needle. Work step 11 of the zig-zag jacquard st across the 18 sts from step 5. Now pick up and k 32 sts along the second side of the rectangle until you reach the bottom left corner of the cast on. (82 sts.)

   You are now ready to work back and forth across these sts.

7. (WS) P32, work row 12 of zig-zag jacquard st across 18 sts, p32.

8. Working across all 82 sts, repeat rows 1 to 12 of zig-zag jacquard st a further 6 times. (72 rows.)

9. Repeat rows 1 to 8 of zig-zag jacquard st once more.

   You will now start the neck rib section. Cut color B leaving a 6in yarn tail.

10. (RS) With US 7 (4.5mm) needles and color A, cast on 14 sts at the start of the row using the cable cast on technique. Work across 96 sts as follows: (P2, k2) x 3, p2, *k2tog, k1, p2*, repeat section in stars (*) until 2 sts remain, k2. Place st marker to mark the start of the round and join to work in the round. (80 sts.)

11. *P2, k2*, repeat section in stars until end of round.

12. Repeat step 11, working in 2 x 2 rib stitch until rib measures 4½in.

13. Bind off in 2 x 2 ribbing.

    You will now pick up and k sts around the hood opening to knit the rib trim.

14. With US 7 (4.5mm) needles and color A, start at the bottom left of the hood opening and pick up and k 84 sts as follows: Pick up 37 sts until you reach the centre top of the hood, pick up another 37 sts until you reach the cast-on sts. Pick up 10 sts into the cast on, skipping the first and last 2 sts of the 14-st cast on. Place a marker for the start of the round and join to work in the round. (84 sts.)

15. Repeat step 11, working in 2 x 2 rib stitch until the rib measures 1¼in.

16. Bind off in 2 x 2 ribbing.

We recommend you block your hood to even out the stitches and achieve the correct measurements.

The Rush hood is a follow-up to the first ever ROWS pattern—the much loved Bug hood.

Mix up blanket

The Mix up blanket uses a traditional quilting method called the log cabin technique, which has been adapted into knit and crochet.
First, a central rectangle is knitted and then bind off. Stitches are then picked up along one side of the rectangle to start knitting the next rectangle. You continue to work like this, gradually working outwards in different directions until the design of the blanket is complete. We have used all-over garter stitch stripes to create a structured, geometric design.

Size
One size

Flat measurements
45½ x 72¾in

Yarn
Worsted-weight yarn. For each rectangle of stripes, the light color in the stripe is referred to as color A and the darker color as color B. Here is the approx. yarn usage for each rectangle:

R1: Color A – 79yds/72m, **color B** – 69yds/63m

R2: Color A – 153yds/140m, **color B** – 122yds/112m

R3: Color A – 230yds/210m, **color B** – 197yds/180m

R4: Color A – 164yds/150m, **color B** – 126yds/115m

R5: Color A – 219yds/200m, **color B** – 241yds/220m

R6: Color A – 230yds/210m, **color B** – 184yds/168m

R7: Color A – 227yds/208m, **color B** – 230yds/210m

R8: Color A – 192yds/176m, **color B** – 137yds/125m.

R9: Color A – 105yds/96m

R10: Color A – 61yds/56m

R11: Color A – 114yds/104m

R12: Color A – 69yds/63m

We mostly used yarn from our stash for this project, but here are some suggested yarns for this pattern:
Wool and the Gang The One Merino, Fonty Tartan 6, Drops Alaska, Drops Nepal, Lana Grossa Bingo

Recommended needles
US 8 (5mm) circular knitting needles, length 47in. You will be working flat, but as the rectangles get bigger, you will need the length of a circular needle.

Gauge
Garter stitch unblocked US 8 (5 mm) needles:
4 x 4in = 17 stitches x 34 rows

Knitting notes

- The diagram below shows the placement of each rectangle. The measurements are shown as width x height. The arrows show the direction of the stripes as well as the edge the stitches are cast on/picked up.

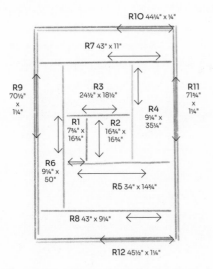

R10 44¼" x ¼"

R7 43" x 11"

R9 70½" x 1¼"

R3 24½" x 18½"

R11 71¾" x 1¼"

R4 9¼" x 35¼"

R1 7¾" x 16¾"

R2 16¾" x 16¾"

R6 9¼" x 50"

R5 34" x 14¾"

R8 43" x 9¼"

R12 45½" x 1¼"

- When picking up stitches always make sure the RS is facing upwards.
- When picking up stitches on garter stitch rows, pick up a stitch every other row, only working into the flat rows of the pattern, in between each ridge.
- When picking up sts on a bound-off or cast-on edge, pick up a stitch into every stitch.
- For each stripe, make sure you always change color on a RS row.
- Make sure the bind off for each rectangle is not too tight.
- We steam blocked each rectangle along the way to keep it looking neat.

Garter stitch

Instructions

Rectangle 1 (R1)

1. With color A, cast on 36 sts using the long tail cast on technique.

2. K 15 rows.

3. With color B, k 16 rows.

4. With color A, k 16 rows.

5. Repeat steps 3 and 4 a further 3 times. You should now have 9 stripes.

6. Bind off.

Rectangle 2 (R2)

1. Rotate work R1 90 degrees anti-clockwise. With color A pick up and k 74 sts along the top edge.

2. K 15 rows.

3. Repeat steps 3 and 4 of R1 a further 4 times. You should now have 9 stripes.

4. Bind off.

Rectangle 3 (R3)

1. Rotate work 90 degrees clockwise from R2 cast-off position. With color A pick up and k 108 sts along the top edge.

2. K 15 rows.

3. Repeat steps 3 and 4 of R1 a further 4 times.

4. With color B, k 16 rows. You should now have 10 stripes.

5. Bind off.

Rectangle 4 (R4)

1. Rotate work 90 degrees anti-clockwise from R3 cast-off position. With color A pick up and k 154 sts along the top edge.

2. K 15 rows.

3. Repeat steps 3 and 4 of R1 twice more. You should now have 5 stripes.

4. Bind off.

Rectangle 5 (R5)

1. Rotate work 90 degrees anti-clockwise from R4 cast-off position. With color A pick up and k 148 sts along the top edge.

2. K 15 rows.

3. Repeat steps 3 and 4 of R1 a further 3 times.

4. With color B, k 16 rows. You should now have 8 stripes.

5. Bind off.

Rectangle 6 (R6)

1. Rotate work 90 degrees anti-clockwise from R5 cast-off position. With color A pick up and k 218 sts along the top edge.

2. K 15 rows.

3. Repeat steps 3 and 4 of R1 twice more. You should now have 5 stripes.

4. Bind off.

Rectangle 7 (R7)

1. Rotate work 90 degrees anti-clockwise from R6 cast-off position. With color A pick up and k 188 sts along the top edge.

2. K 15 rows.

3. Repeat steps 3 and 4 of R1 twice more.

4. With color B, k 16 rows. You should now have 6 stripes.

5. Bind off.

Rectangle 8 (R8)

1. Rotate work 180 degrees from R7 cast-off position. With color A pick up and k 188 sts along the top edge.

2. K 15 rows.

3. Repeat steps 3 and 4 of R1 twice more. You should now have 5 stripes.

4. Bind off.

Rectangle 9 (R9)

1. Rotate work 90 degrees anti-clockwise from R8 cast-off position. With color A pick up and k 306 sts along the top edge.

2. K 9 rows.

3. Bind off.

Rectangle 10 (R10)

1. Rotate work 90 degrees anti-clockwise from R9 bound-off position. With color A pick up and k 193 sts along the top edge. Make sure you pick up sts at the very edges.

2. Sl1p, k until end of row.

3. Repeat step 2 a further 8 times.

4. Bind off.

Rectangle 11 (R11)

1. Rotate work 90 degrees anti-clockwise from R10 bound-off position. With color A pick up and k 311 sts along the top edge. Make sure you pick up sts at the very edges.

2. Repeat steps 2 to 4 of R10.

Rectangle 12 (R12)

1. Rotate work 90 degrees anti-clockwise from R11 bound-off position. With color A pick up and k 198 sts along the top edge. Make sure you pick up sts at the very edges.

2. Repeat steps 2 to 4 of R10.

3. Weave in loose ends.

This was a great project to use up stash yarn. A version striping the same
two colors throughout is also on our knit list.

Ziggy sweater

The Ziggy sweater is designed with a cropped fit, tight 1 x 1 rib trims and a button-up neckline. The texture is created by using long slip stripe stitch in four colors and a mix of yarn weights. The sweater is knitted in the round from the bottom up to the armholes, where the stitches are split in half, working the front and back separately flat. The shoulder seams are joined, and then stitches are picked up to form the neck rib and front plackets. Finally, stitches are picked up around the armholes to knit the sleeves from the top down.

Size
This pattern includes 8 sizes; see page 150 for size chart. Sana wears size 2.

Flat measurements

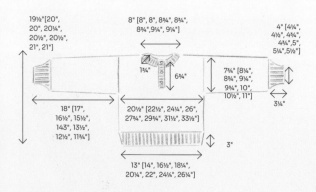

19½"[20", 20", 20¼", 20½", 20½", 21", 21"]

8" [8", 8", 8¾", 8¾", 8¾",9¼", 9¼"]

4" [4¼", 4½", 4¾", 4¾",5", 5¼",5½"]

1¾"

6¾"

7¾" [8¼", 8¾", 9¼", 9¾", 10", 10½", 11"]

3¼"

18" [17", 16½", 15½", 14¾", 13½", 12½", 11¾"]

20½" [22½", 24¼", 26", 27¾", 29¾", 31½", 33½"]

3"

13" [14", 16½", 18¼", 20¼", 22, 24¼", 26¼"]

Yarn
Using a mix of yarn weights and textures gives the most interesting result for this stitch.

We used
Fingering weight yarn (color A), two worsted weight yarns (colors B and D), and one lace weight yarn (color C):

Color A + held double for ribs – Brown (we suggest using a darker color)
5 [6, 6, 7, 7, 7, 8, 8] balls of Majo Garn Fine Merino in Brownie – 100% Merino wool (191yds/175m per 50g ball)
Alternative yarn suggestions: Drops Baby Merino, Lana Grossa Cool Wool, Sandnes Garn Tynn Merinoull

Color B – Light gray (we suggest using a lighter color)
4 [5, 5, 5, 6, 6, 6, 6] balls of Scheepjes, Cahlista in color 172 Light Silver – 100% cotton (93yds/85m per 50g ball)
Alternative yarn suggestions: Rico Creative Cotton Aran, Cascade Yarns Nifty Cotton, Quince & Co Whimbrel

Color C – Dark gray (we suggest using a darker color)
2 [2, 3, 3, 3, 3, 4, 4] balls of Scheepjes Maxi Sweet Treat in color 393 Charcoal – 100% cotton mercerized (153yds/140m per 25g ball)
Alternative yarn suggestions: Hobbii Rainbow Lace, Isager Trio 1, Knitting for Olive Pure Silk

Color D – White (we suggest using a lighter color)

3 [3, 3, 4, 4, 4, 4, 5] balls of CaMaRose Lamauld in color 6000 Råhvid – 50% llama wool, 50% Peruvian highland wool (109yds/100m per 50g ball)

Alternative yarn suggestions: Kremke Soul Wool The Merry Merino 110, Knitting for Olive Heavy Merino, Drops Big Merino

Extras

You will need 3 x ¾in buttons.

Recommended needles

US 4 (3.5mm) circular knitting needles, length 32–40in

US 8 (5mm) circular knitting needles, length 16–20in and 40–55in

Gauge

Long Slip Stripe Stitch (see page 36) after blocking on US 8 (5mm) needles:

4 x 4in = 26 stitches x 42 rows

1 x 1 rib after blocking on US 4 (3.5mm) needles using 2 strands of color A:

4 x 4in = 26 stitches x 34 rows

Knitting notes

- After binding off, 1 st is always left on the right needle. For this pattern, any instructions after the bind off only apply to the sts on the left needle.
- For this pattern when sl1p (slip 1 purlwise) is mentioned, if you are on the right side of the work keep yarn at the back, if you are on the wrong side keep yarn at the front.
- Please refer to the charts on pages 164–7 when referenced in the instructions.

Long slip stripe stitch

Instructions

Body

1. With US 4 (3.5mm) needles and 2 strands of color A, cast on 172 [188, 216, 240, 266, 294, 320, 346] sts using the long tail cast on technique.

   Place a stitch marker to mark the start of the round and join to work in the round, being careful not to twist your sts.

2. *P1, k1*, repeat section in stars (*) until end of round.

3. Repeat step 2 until your piece measures 3in from the cast-on edge (approx. 24 more rounds).

Sizes 1, 4, 7 and 8 only:

4. With US 8 (5mm) needles, length 40–55in and 1 strand of color A, k3 [k0, k0, k0], *k1 [k2, k3, k3], m1, k2 [k3, k4, k4], m1, k2 [k2, k3, k4], m1*, repeat section in stars until 4 [2, 0, 5] sts remain, k2 [k1, k0, k4], m1 [m1, m0, m1], k2 [k1, k0, k1], m0 [m1, m0, m0]. (272 [344, 416, 440] sts.)

Size 2 only:

5. With US 8 (5mm) needles, length 40–55in and 1 strand of color A, *k1, m1, k2, m1, k1, m1, k3, m1*, repeat section in stars until 6 sts remain, k1, m1, k2, m1, k1, m1, k1, m1, k1. (296 sts.)

Sizes 3, 5 and 6 only:

6. With US 8 (5mm) needles, length 40–55in and 1 strand of color A, [k4, k5, k0], *[k2, k2, k3], m1, [k0, k3, k0], [m0, m1, m0]*, repeat section in stars until [4, 6, 0] sts remain, [k4, k6, k0]. ([320, 368, 392] sts.)

All sizes:

7. Repeat steps 1 to 6 of long slip stripe stitch worked in the round (see page 36) until your piece measures 1½in [11½in, 11¼in, 10¾in, 10¾in, 10½in, 10½in, 10in] from the cast-on edge. Make sure last round worked is the end of step 2 using color D [D, C, B, B, A, A, D]. (5 [5, 5, 5, 5, 4, 4, 4] full repeats + 11 [11, 7, 3, 3, 15, 15, 11] rounds. (91 [91, 87, 83, 83, 79, 79, 75] rounds in total.)

8. With color D [D, C, B, B, A, A, D], k135 [147, 159, 171, 183, 195, 207, 219], k1fb, turn your work. (137 [149, 161, 173, 185, 197, 209, 221] sts.)

   You will now be working flat over these sts only to make the back of your sweater.

Sizes 1, 2, 3, 4, 5, and 8 only:

9. Work steps 7 [7, 6–7, 5–7, 5–7, 7] of long slip stripe stitch worked flat. (4 [4, 8, 12, 12, 4] rows in total.)

All sizes:

10. Repeat steps 1 to 7 of long slip stripe stitch worked flat until your piece measures 18¾in [19¼in, 19¼in, 19½in, 20in, 20in, 20¼in, 20¼in] from the cast-on edge. Make sure last row worked is the end of step 4 using color D [D, D, A, B, B, C, C]. (4 [4, 4, 5, 5, 6, 6, 6] full repeats + 8 [12, 12, 0, 4, 4, 8, 8] rows. (72 [76, 76, 80, 84, 100, 104, 104] rows in total.)

11. (WS) With color D [A, A, B, C, C, D, D], *p1, sl1p*, repeat section in stars until you have worked 44 [50, 56, 60, 66, 72, 76, 82] sts, p1. Turn your work. (45 [51, 57, 61, 67, 73, 77, 83] sts.)

    You will now be working over these sts only to make one half of the back neck. (You will come back to the other sts later.)

12. Ssk, *k1, sl1p*, repeat section in stars until 1 st remains, k1. (44 [50, 56, 60, 66, 72, 76, 82] sts.)

13. *P1, sl1p*, repeat section in stars until 2 sts remain, p2.

14. Ssk, k until the end of the row. (43 [49, 55, 59, 65, 71, 75, 81] sts.)

15. Using color A [B, B, C, D, D, A, A] work steps 1 to 3 of long slip stripe stitch worked flat.

16. Bind off. If you are using colors A or C, make sure you bind off loosely throughout or use colors B or D instead.

17. WS facing outwards, re-join color D [A, A, B, C, C, D, D] to 92 [98, 104, 112, 118, 124, 132, 138] sts waiting on your needle. Bind off purlwise 47 [47, 47, 51, 51, 51, 55, 55] sts. *Sl1p, p1*, repeat section in stars until end of row. (45 [51, 57, 61, 67, 73, 77, 83] sts.)

18. *K1, sl1p*, repeat section in stars until 3 sts remain, k1, k2tog. (44 [50, 56, 60, 66, 72, 76, 82] sts.)

19. P1, *p1, sl1p*, repeat section in stars until 1 st remains, p1.

20. K until 2 sts remain, k2tog. (43 [49, 55, 59, 65, 71, 75, 81] sts.)

21. Repeat steps 15 and 16 once more.

22. RS facing outwards, re-join color D [D, C, B, B, A, A, D] to 136 [148, 160, 172, 184, 196, 208, 220] sts waiting on your needle for the sweater front. K until 1 st remains, k1fb. (137 [149, 161, 173, 185, 197, 209, 221] sts.)

Sizes 1, 2 and 8 only:

23. With color A work steps 1–2 [1–4, 1–4] of long slip stripe stitch worked flat. (2 [4, 4] rows in total.)

Sizes 3, 4, 5, 6, 7 and 8 only:

24. Work steps [6–7, 5–7, 5–7, 1–7, 1–7, 1–7] of long slip stripe stitch worked flat. ([8, 12, 12, 16, 16, 16] rows in total.)

Sizes 5 and 7 only:

25. With color B work steps [1–2, 1–2] of long slip stripe stitch worked flat. ([2, 2] rows in total.)

All sizes:

26. (WS) With color A [B, B, B, B, B, B, B], *p1, sl1p*. repeat section in stars until you have worked 64 [70, 76, 82, 88, 94, 100, 106] sts, p1. Turn your work. You will now be working over these 65 [71, 77, 83, 89, 95, 101, 107] sts only to make one half of the front.

Size 1 only:

27. With color A, k all sts.

Sizes 2, 3, 4, 5, 6, 7 and 8 only:

28. Work steps [2–7, 2–7, 2–7, 4–7, 2–7, 4–7, 2–7] of long slip stripe stitch worked flat. ([15, 15, 15, 13, 15, 13, 15] rows in total.)

All sizes:

29. Repeat steps 1 to 7 of long slip stripe stitch worked flat until the left half of the front measures 5in from step 26. Make sure last row worked is step 3 [1, 1, 1, 3, 1, 3, 1] using color B [C, C, C, C, C, C, C]. (3 [2, 2, 2, 2, 2, 2, 2] full repeats + 3 [5, 5, 5, 7, 5, 7, 5] rows. 51 [37, 37, 37, 39, 37, 39, 37] rows in total.)

Sizes 1, 5 and 7 only:

30. (RS) With color B [C, C] bind off 7 sts, k until the end of the row. (58 [82, 94] sts.)

Sizes 2, 3, 4, 6 and 8 only:

31. (RS) With color C bind off 7 sts. *K1, sl1p*, repeat section in stars until 1 st remains, k1. ([64, 70, 76, 88, 100] sts.)

All sizes:

32. Starting with row 1 (WS row) follow the left front chart until you finish the chart. (43 [49, 55, 59, 65, 71, 75, 81] sts.) Follow only the chart for your size.

33. Bind off.

34. WS facing outwards, re-join color A [B, B, B, B, B, B, B] to 72 [78, 84, 90, 96, 102, 108, 114] sts waiting on your needle. Bind off 7 sts. *Sl1p, p1*, repeat section in stars until end of row. (65 [71, 77, 83, 89, 95, 101, 107] sts.)

35. Repeat steps 27 and 28 once more, following only the steps for your size.

36. Repeat steps 1 to 7 of long slip stripe st worked flat until the right half of the front measures 5in from step 34. Make sure last row worked is step 2 [4, 4, 4, 2, 4, 2, 4] using color B [B, B, B, C, B, C, B].

(3 [2, 2, 2, 2, 2, 2, 2] full repeats + 2 [4, 4, 4, 6, 4, 6, 4] rows. 50 [36, 36, 36, 38, 36, 38, 36] rows in total.)

37. (WS) With color B [C, C, C, C, C, C, C], bind off 7 sts. *P1, sl1p*, repeat section in stars until 1 st remains, p1. (58 [64, 70, 76, 82, 88, 94, 100] sts.)

38. Starting with row 1 (RS row) follow the right front chart until you finish the chart. (43 [49, 55, 59, 65, 71, 75, 81] sts.)

39. Bind off.

40. RS facing outwards, use the horizontal invisible seam technique to sew the front and back shoulder seams together.

Neck rib

1. RS facing outwards, with 2 strands of color A held together and US 4 (3.5mm) needles, pick up and k 95 [95, 95, 103, 107, 107, 115, 119] sts in total around the neckline. Start at front left neck point and work from right to left as follows:

   Pick up 26 [26, 26, 28, 30, 30, 32, 34] sts around the front left neck until you reach the shoulder seam, pick up 43 [43, 43, 47, 47, 47, 51, 51] sts around the back neck until you reach the second shoulder seam, then pick up 26 [26, 26, 28, 30, 30, 32, 34] sts around the front right neck. (95 [95, 95, 103, 107, 107, 115, 119] sts.)

2. (WS) *k1, p1*, repeat section in stars until 1 st remains, k1.

3. *P1, k1*, repeat section in stars until 1 st remains, p1.

4. Repeat steps 2 and 3 until your rib measures 3½in. Make sure last row is a WS row (approx. 29 more rows).

5. Bind off using the folded bind off technique, folding the RS of trim over to connect it to the edge you picked up the sts from step 1.

Front plackets

1. RS facing outwards, with 2 strands of color A held together and US 4 (3.5mm) needles, pick up and k 44 sts in total. Start at the top of the front right neck rib and work from right to left down the front opening. Make sure you go through both layers of the neck trim. (44 sts.)

2. (WS) *k1, p1*, repeat section in stars until end of row.

3. Sl1k, *p1, k1*, repeat section in stars until 1 st remains, p1.

4. Repeat steps 2 and 3 until your rib measures 1½in from the cast-on edge. Make sure last row is a WS row (approx. 9 more rows).

5. Bind off in ribbing.

6. RS facing outwards, start at the bottom of the front left neck opening, work from right to left repeating step 1. (44 sts.)

7. (WS) sl1p, *k1, p1*, repeat section in stars until 1 st remains, k1.

8. *P1, k1*, repeat section in stars until end of row.

9. Repeat steps 7 and 8 until your rib measures ½in. Make sure last row is a WS row (approx. 3 more rows).

Now you will make the buttonholes.

10. (RS) (p1, k1) x 4, p1, bind off 3 sts. *(K1, p1) x 5, bind off 3 sts*, repeat section in stars once more, k1, p1, k1. (35 sts.)

11. Sl1p, k1, p1, k1, turn work and cast on 3 sts using the cable cast on, turn work back. *(K1, p1) x 5, k1, turn work and cast on 3 sts using the cable cast on, turn work back.* Repeat section in stars once more. (K1, p1) x 4, k1. (44 sts.)

12. Starting with step 8, repeat steps 7 and 8 until your rib measures 1½in. Make sure last row is a WS row (approx. 4 more rows).

13. Bind off in ribbing.

14. Use the perpendicular invisible seam technique to join the bottom of the right placket to the sts bind off on the body.

15. Sew 3 buttons to the centre of the right placket as follows: Sew button 1 so the centre sits ¾in from the top, sew button 2 so the centre sits 2in from the centre of button 1 and sew button 3 so the centre sits 2in from the centre of button 2.

16. Repeat step 14 for the bottom of the left placket, sewing it on top of the right placket.

Sleeves

Repeat these instructions twice to make the left and right sleeves.

1. RS facing outwards, use color B [D, B, D, B, B, D, B] and US 8 (5mm) needles, length 16–20in to pick up and k 104 [110, 114, 124, 128, 134, 140, 144] sts in total around the armhole. Start at the underarm point and work from right to left as follows:

   Pick up 52 [55, 57, 62, 64, 67, 70, 72] sts from the underarm point to shoulder seam, then 52 [55, 57, 62, 64, 67, 70, 72] sts from shoulder seam to underarm point. (104 [110, 114, 124, 128, 134, 140, 144] sts.)

   Place a stitch marker to mark the start of the round and join to work in the round.

2. K 1 round.

3. Work steps 4–6 [6, 4–6, 6, 4–6, 4–6, 6, 4–6] of long slip stripe stitch worked in the round. (12 [4, 12, 4, 12, 12, 4, 12] rounds in total).

4. Repeat steps 1 to 6 of long slip stripe stitch worked in the round until your sleeve measures 14¾in [14in, 13¼in, 12½in, 11½in, 10¼in, 9½in, 8¾in]. Make sure last round worked is using color A at the end of step 2. (8 [8, 7, 7, 6, 5, 5, 4] full repeats + 15 rounds. 143 [143, 127, 127, 111, 95, 95, 79] rounds in total.)

5. Using 2 strands of color A, *k2tog*, repeat section in stars until 0 [2, 2, 0, 0, 2 , 0, 0] sts remain, k0 [k2, k2, k0, k0, k2, k0, k0]. (52 [56, 58, 62, 64, 68, 70, 72] sts.)

6. Using US 4 (3.5mm) needles, *p1, k1*, repeat section in stars until end of round. You will need to use the magic loop method to work with your circular needles.

7. Repeat step 6 until your cuff measures 3¼in (approx. 25 more rounds).

8. Bind off in ribbing.

9. Weave in loose ends.

We recommend you block your sweater to even out the stitches and achieve the correct measurements.

See page 14 for inspiration on knitting this piece in stash yarn, using a different color for each 4-row stitch repeat.

Striped slip rib stitch

Knit

Off grid top

Knitted in a three-colored stripe slip rib stitch, the Off grid top is a fitted summer cropped top with wide straps. Knitted from the bottom up, the body is worked in the round and then sections are bind off, with two straps knitted flat on the front and two on the back. The tops of the straps are then sewn together.

Size
This pattern includes 8 sizes; see page 150 for size chart. Lydia wears size 2.

Flat measurements
The body width measurements may seem small, but this is taken non-stretched. Due to the nature of the ribbed fabric, there is a large amount of stretch.

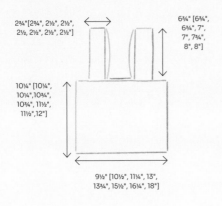

2¾"[2¾", 2½", 2½", 2½", 2½", 2½", 2½"]

6¾" [6¾", 6¾", 7", 7", 7¾", 8", 8"]

10¼" [10¼", 10¼", 10¾", 10¾", 11½", 11½", 12"]

9½" [10½", 11¼", 13", 13¾", 15½", 16¼", 18"]

Yarn
DK weight yarn in 3 colors.
We suggest using a cotton Merino blend to get the elasticity of Merino wool and the coolness of cotton. You will need approx. 104yds/95m [115yds/105m, 126yds/115m, 150yds/137m, 165yds/151m, 196yds/179m, 207yds/189m, 230yds/210m] of colors A and C, and 168yds/154m [192yds/176m, 205yds/187m, 241yds/220m, 265yds/242m, 313yds/286m, 337yds/308m, 385yds/352m] of color B.

We used
Color A – Blue
1 [1, 2, 2, 2, 2, 2, 2] balls of Drops Merino Extra Fine in color 39 Ice Blue - 100% wool (115yds/105m per 50g ball)

Color B – White
2 [2, 2, 2, 3, 3, 3, 4] balls of Drops Cotton Merino in 01 Natural – 50% wool, 50% cotton (120yds/110m per 50g ball)

Color C - Red
1 [1, 2, 2, 2, 2, 2, 2] balls of Knitting For Olive, Cotton Merino in Rust - 70% cotton, 30% wool (273yds/250m per 50g ball). Note this is a fingering weight yarn but we have used 2 strands held together to make a DK weight yarn.
Alternative yarn suggestions: Sandnes Garn Duo, Hjertegarn Merino Cotton, Lang Yarns Merino 120

Recommended needles
US 6 (4mm) circular knitting needles, length 24–32in
2 x US 6 (4mm) double-pointed needles or US 6 (4mm) circular knitting needles, length 16in

Gauge:
Striped slip rib stitch (see page 38) unblocked and not stretched:
4 x 4in = 32 stitches x 32 rows

Knitting notes

- For the straps, two colors alternate each row. To avoid cutting yarns after each row, we suggest using double-pointed or circular needles to work flat. When the next color to be worked is on the opposite side of the needle, slide your stitches to the other side of your circular needle, so that the correct color is ready to start the next row.
- Please refer to the strap charts on pages 168–9 when referenced in the instructions.

Instructions

1. With US 6 (4mm) circular knitting needles, length 24–32in and color A, cast on 154 [168, 182, 210, 224, 252, 266, 294] sts using the long tail cast on technique.

   Place a marker to mark the start of the round and join to work in the round, being careful not to twist your sts.

2. *P3, k1, p1, k1, p1, k1, p3, k3*, repeat section in stars (*) until end of round.

3. With color B, *p3, k1, p1, sl1pwyib, p1, k1, p3, k1, sl1pwyib, k1*, repeat section in stars until end of round.

4. With color A, *p3, sl1pwyib, p1, k1, p1, sl1pwyib, p3, k3*, repeat section in stars until end of round.

5. Repeat steps 3 and 4 a further 6 [6, 6, 6, 6, 7, 7, 7] times (12 [12, 12, 12, 12, 14, 14, 14] rounds).

6. With colors B and C, repeat steps 3 and 4 a further 9 [9, 9, 10, 10, 10, 10, 11] times. When color A is mentioned, replace with color C. (18 [18, 18, 20, 20, 20, 20, 22] rounds.)

7. With colors A and B, repeat steps 3 and 4 a further 8 [8, 8, 8, 8, 9, 9, 9] times (16 [16, 16, 16, 16, 18, 18, 18] rounds).

8. Repeat step 6 once more. (18 [18, 18, 20, 20, 20, 20, 22] rounds.)

9. With colors A and B, repeat steps 3 and 4 a further 7 [7, 7, 7, 7, 8, 8, 8] times. (14 [14, 14, 14, 14, 16, 16, 16] rounds.)

10. Repeat step 3 once more.

Sizes 1, 3, 4 and 7 only:

11. With color A, *p3, sl1pwyib, p1, k1, p1, sl1pwyib, p3, k3*, repeat section in stars once more. °P3, k1, p1, k1, p1, k1, p3, k3°. Repeat section in stars (*) twice more. Repeat section in circles (°) a further 1 [2, 3, 5] times. Repeat section in stars once more. Repeat section in circles twice more. Repeat section in stars once more. Repeat section in circles a further 1 [2, 3, 5] times.

Sizes 2, 5, 6 and 8 only:

12. With color A, *p3, k1, p1, k1, p1, k1, p3, k3*, °p3, sl1pwyib, p1, k1, p1, sl1pwyib, p3, k3°, repeat section in circles (°) once more. Repeat section in stars (*) once more. Repeat section in circles twice more. Repeat section in stars a further [1, 3, 4, 6] times. Repeat section in circles a further [2, 2, 2, 1] times. Repeat section in stars a further [1, 1, 1, 2] times. Repeat section in circles a further [2, 2, 2, 1] times. Repeat section in stars a further [0, 2, 3, 5] times.

All sizes:

13. With color A, sl1pwyib [sl0, sl2pwyib, sl2pwyib, sl0, sl0, sl0, sl0], bind off 0 [15, 0, 0, 15, 14, 0, 13] sts in ribbing. With color B, p2 [p2, p1, p1, p2, p3, p3, p4],

k1, p1, sl1pwyib, p1, k1, p3, k1, sl1pwyib, k1, p3, k1, p1, sl1pwyib [sl1pwyib, sl1pwyib, sl1pwyib, sl1pwyib, sl1pwyib, sl1pwyib, sl0], p1, k1 [k1, k1, k1, k1, k0, k0, k0], p2 [p2, p1, p1, p0, p0, p0, p0]. Turn your work.

You will now be working back and forth over these 23 [23, 21, 21, 21, 21, 21, 21] sts only to form one strap. Swap to US 6 (4mm) dpn or circular needles, length 16in.

14. With colors B and C, work rows 1 to 5 of the strap 1 chart, remember to follow the chart for your size. When the next color worked is on the opposite side of the needle, slide the sts to the other side of your needle to start the next row. Work like this for each strap.

15. Repeat rows 2 to 5 of the strap 1 chart a further 3 [3, 3, 4, 4, 4, 4, 4] times. (12 [12, 12, 16, 16, 16, 16, 16] rows.)

16. With colors A and B, repeat rows 2 to 5 of the strap 1 chart a further 4 [4, 4, 4, 4, 5, 5, 5] times. When it shows color C on the chart, replace with color A. (16 [16, 16, 16, 16, 20, 20, 20] rows.)

17. With colors B and C, repeat rows 2 to 5 of the strap 1 chart a further 5 times. (20 rows.)

Sizes 7 and 8 only:
18. Repeat rows 2 and 3 of the strap 1 chart once more. (2 rows.)

All sizes:
19. Bind off.

Note, instead of binding off, at this point you can put the sts on a stitch holder so that you can easily shorten or lengthen the straps later on.

20. RS facing outwards, rejoin color A to sts waiting on your needle. Bind off 19 [19, 21, 21, 23, 25, 25, 27] sts in ribbing. With color B, p2 [p2, p1, p1, p0, p0, p0, p0], k1 [k1, k1, k1, k1, k0, k0, k0], p1 [p1, p1, p1, p1, p1, p1, p0], sl1pwyib, p1, k1, p3, k1, sl1pwyib, k1, p3, k1, p1, sl1pwyib, p1, k1, p2 [p2, p1, p1, p2, p3, p3, p4]. Turn your work.

You will now be working back and forth over these 23 [23, 21, 21, 21, 21, 21] sts only to form the second strap. Again swap to US 6 (4mm) dpn or circular needles, length 16in.

Sizes 1, 3 and 4 only:
21. Repeat steps 14 to 19 once more.

22. RS facing outwards, rejoin color A to sts waiting on your needle. Bind off 12 [28, 42] sts in ribbing. With color B, p3 [p2, p2], k1, sl1pwyib, k1, p3, k1, p1, sl1pwyib, p1, k1, p3, k1, sl1pwyib, k1, p3 [p2, p2]. Turn your work.

You will now be working back and forth over these 23 [21, 21] sts only to form the third strap. Again swap to US 6 (4mm) dpn needles or circular needles, length 16in.

23. With colors B and C, work rows 1 to 5 of the strap 2 chart.

24. Repeat rows 2 to 5 of the strap 2 chart a further 3 [3, 4] times. (12 [12, 16] rows.)

25. With colors A and B, repeat rows 2 to 5 of the strap 2 chart a further 4 times. When it shows color C on the chart, replace with color A. (16 rows.)

26. With colors B and C, repeat rows 2 to 5 of the strap 2 chart a further 5 times. (20 rows.)

27. Bind off.

28. RS facing outwards, rejoin color A to sts waiting on your needle. Bind off 19 [21, 21] sts in ribbing. With color B, p3 [p2, p2], k1, sl1pwyib, k1, p3, k1, p1, sl1pwyib, p1, k1, p3, k1, sl1pwyib, k1, p3 [p2, p2]. Turn your work.

   You will now be working back and forth over these 23 [21, 21] sts only to form the fourth strap. Again swap to US 6 (4mm) dpn or circular needles, length 16in.

29. Repeat steps 23 to 27 once more.

30. RS facing outwards, rejoin color A to sts waiting on your needle. Bind off remaining 12 [28, 42] sts in ribbing. Skip to step 61.

Size 2 only:

31. Repeat steps 14 to 20 twice more.

32. Repeat steps 14 to 19 once more.

33. RS facing outwards, rejoin color A to sts waiting on your needle. Bind off remaining 4 sts in ribbing. Skip to step 61.

Sizes 5, 6, 7 and 8 only:

34. With colors B and C, work rows 1 to 5 of the strap 2 chart.

35. Repeat rows 2 to 5 of the strap 2 chart a further 4 times. (16 rows.)

36. With colors A and B, repeat rows 2 to 5 of the strap 2 chart a further [4, 5, 5, 5] times. When it shows color C on the chart, replace with color A. ([16, 20, 20, 20] rows.)

37. With colors B and C, repeat rows 2 to 5 of the strap 2 chart a further 5 times. (20 rows.)

Sizes 5 and 6 only:

38. Bind off.

39. RS facing outwards, rejoin color A to sts waiting on your needle. Bind off [47, 59] sts in ribbing. With color B, [p2, p3], k1, p1, sl1pwyib, p1, k1, p3, k1, sl1pwyib, k1, p3, k1, p1, sl1pwyib, p1, [k1, k0]. Turn your work.

   You will now be working back and forth over these 21 sts only to form the third strap. Again swap to US 6 (4mm) dpn or circular needles, length 16in.

40. Repeat steps 14 to 20 once more.

41. Repeat steps 34 to 38 once more

42. RS facing outwards, rejoin color A to sts waiting on your needle. Bind off remaining [32, 45] sts in ribbing. Skip to step 61.

Size 7 and 8 only:

43. Repeat rows 2 and 3 of the strap 2 chart once more. (2 rows.)

44. Bind off.

45. RS facing outwards, rejoin color A to sts waiting on your needle. Bind off [66, 78] sts in ribbing. With color B, p1, [k0, k1], p3, k1, sl1pwyib, k1, p3, k1, p1, sl1pwyib, p1, k1, p3, [k1, k2], [sl1pwyib, sl0], [k1, k0]. Turn your work.

   You will now be working back and forth over these 21 sts only to form the third strap. Again swap to US 6 (4mm) dpn or circular needles, length 16in.

46. With colors B and C, work rows 1 to 5 of the strap 3 chart.

47. Repeat rows 2 to 5 of the strap 3 chart a further 4 times. (16 rows.)

48. With colors A and B, repeat rows 2 to 5 of the strap 3 chart a further 5 times. When it shows color C on the chart, replace with color A. (20 rows.)

49. With colors B and C, repeat rows 2 to 5 of the strap 3 chart a further 5 times. (20 rows.)

50. Repeat rows 2 and 3 of the strap 3 chart once more. (2 rows.)

51. Bind off.

52. RS facing outwards, rejoin color A to sts waiting on your needle. Bind off [25, 27] sts in ribbing. With color B, k1, [sl1pwyib, sl0], k1, p3, k1, p1, sl1pwyib, p1, k1, p3, k1, sl1pwyib, k1, p3, k1, [p0, p1]. Turn your work.

    You will now be working back and forth over these 21 sts only to form the fourth strap. Again swap to US 6 (4mm) dpn or circular needles, length 16in.

53. With colors B and C, work rows 1 to 5 of the strap 4 chart.

54. Repeat rows 2 to 5 of the strap 4 chart a further 4 times. (16 rows.)

55. With colors A and B, repeat rows 2 to 5 of the strap 4 chart a further 5 times. When it shows color C on the chart, replace with color A. (20 rows.)

56. With colors B and C, repeat rows 2 to 5 of the strap 4 chart a further 5 times. (20 rows.)

57. Repeat rows 2 and 3 of the strap 4 chart once more. (2 rows.)

58. Bind off.

59. RS facing outwards, rejoin color A to sts waiting on your needle. Bind off remaining [66, 65] sts in ribbing.

All sizes:

60. To finish, use the invisible horizontal seam technique to sew the tops of the front and back straps together. If you didn't bind off the straps, try the top on and check the length, adjust, then bind off and seam together.

61. Weave in all loose ends, neatening up the neck and armholes. We don't recommend blocking the top to keep the elasticity. However, we steam blocked the straps so that they sit flat on the body.

The sister to one of our first patterns, the Off grid sweater, this pattern was the catalyst for many of our other slip stitch designs.

Echo scarf

Knitted in basket rib stitch, the Echo scarf uses three colors and a mix of yarn weights. The cast on is at one end of the scarf, then basket rib stitch is worked alongside slipped edge stitches until the desired length is reached.

Size
One size

Flat measurements

9.5"

65"

Yarn
We used one DK weight yarn (color A), one worsted weight yarn (color B), and one fingering weight yarn (color C):

Color A – Purple
2 balls of CaMaRose Økologisk Hverdagsuld in color 41 Mørk Lilla – 100% organic wool (164yds/150m per 50g ball)
Alternative yarn suggestions: Drops Karisma, BC Garn Semilla

Color B – White
3 balls of Lana Grossa Bingo in color 005 - 100% Merino wool (87yds/80m per 50g ball)
Alternative yarn suggestions: Drops Big Merino, Lang Yarns Merino+, CaMaRose Lamauld

Color C – Blue
2 balls of Lana Grossa Cool Wool in color 2103 – 100% Merino wool (175yds/160m per 50g ball)
Alternative yarn suggestions: Drops Baby Merino, Lang Yarns Merino 150

Recommended needles
US 8 (5mm) knitting needles

Gauge
Basket rib stitch (see page 40) after blocking:
4 x 4in = 19 stitches x 36 rows

Basket rib stitch

Instructions

Work 1 row each in colors A, B, and C throughout. Please refer to basket rib stitch information on page 40 when referenced in the instructions.

1. With color A, cast on 47 sts using the long tail cast on technique.

2. (WS) With color A, sl1p, p all sts.

3. Repeat rows 1 to 4 of basket rib stitch (see page 40) until your scarf measures 65in or the desired length. Make sure last row worked is row 2 of the pattern using color C.

4. With color A, bind off.

5. Weave in loose ends.

   We recommend you block your scarf to relax the stitches and help the side edges sit flat.

This is a great project to substitute one color for leftover yarn, see page 15 for inspiration.

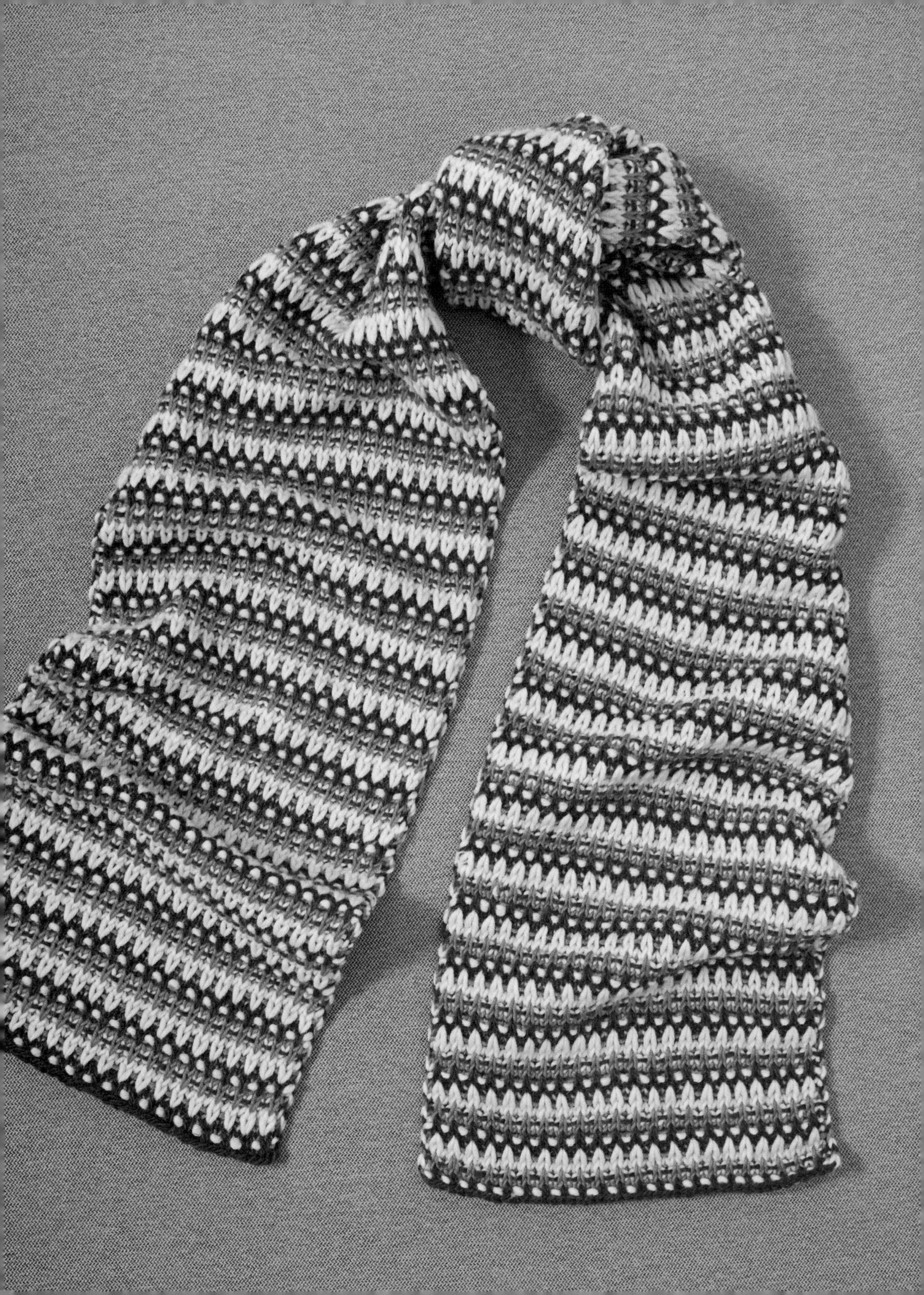

Scrappy cushion

The Scrappy cushion uses the thrumming technique (see page 16) to use up small scraps of yarn left over from past projects. The cushion cover is knitted in the round, then one end is sewn together. The cushion is then inserted, and the other end is sewn together. We have used the smooth knit side as the inside and the tassel yarn ends as the outside of the cushion.

Size
To fit a 20 x 20in cushion.

Flat measurements

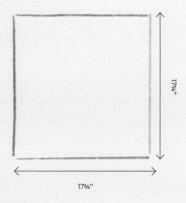

17¾"

17¾"

Yarn
Bulky weight yarn, approx.110yds/100m per 100g. You will need approx. 306yds/280m.

We used
3 balls of Wool and the Gang Alpachino Merino in Sahara Dust – 60% Merino wool, 40% baby alpaca (110yds/100m per 100g ball)

Alternative yarn suggestions: Drops Andes, Fonty Pole, Cascade Yarns 128 Superwash, Drops Alaska, Cascade 220

You will also need approx. 7oz of scrap yarn, based on using mixed weight scrap yarn of approx. 5½in in length.

Recommended needles
US 10.5 (6.5mm) circular knitting needles, length 32in

Gauge
Thrumming unblocked on stockinette stitch: 4 x 4in = 11 stitches x 18 rows

Thrumming on stockinette stitch

Instructions

1. With the main yarn, cast on 100 sts using the long tail cast on technique.

   Place a stitch marker to mark the start of the round and join to work in the round, being careful not to twist your sts.

2. K 3 rounds.

3. *K1, thrum 1 st*, repeat section in stars (*) until end of round.

4. K 1 round.

5. *Thrum 1 st, k1*, repeat section in stars until end of round.

6. K 1 round.

7. Repeat steps 3 to 6 until your cushion measures 17¾in. Make sure last round is a k round (step 4 or step 6).

8. Bind off while working the next thrumming row in sequence (step 5 or step 1). Leave a long yarn tail to sew the end together.

9. Turn your cushion cover so the yarn ends are on the outside, thread your needle with the yarn tail from step 8 and use whip stitch to sew the ends together. Catch scrap yarn into the whip stitch to keep the thrums going right to the edge of the cushion.

10. Insert your cushion, then repeat step 9 to sew the second end together.

If you prefer, you can use the yarn ends as the inside of the cushion and have the smooth side on the outside.

Sol top

The Sol top is a classic tank top knitted from the bottom up in stockinette stitch. We have used two yarns held together throughout to create a variegated marl effect. The top is knitted in the round to the armholes, then the stitches are split in half to work the front and back separately flat. Stitches are then picked up around the armholes and cast on for the straps, which are knitted in stockinette stitch in the round and bind off while folding the trim in half.

Size

This pattern includes 8 sizes; see page 150 for size chart. Sana wears size 2. If you are in between sizes and want a fitted look, we suggest going down a size.

Flat measurements

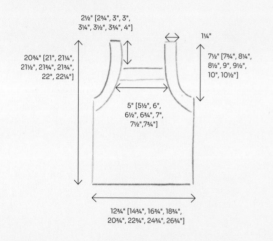

2½" [2¾", 3", 3", 3¼", 3½", 3¾", 4"]

1¼"

20¾" [21", 21¼", 21½", 21¾", 21¾", 22", 22¼"]

7½" [7¾", 8¼", 8½", 9", 9½", 10", 10½"]

5" [5½", 6", 6½", 6¾", 7", 7½", 7¾"]

12¾" [14¾", 16¾", 18¾", 20¾", 22¾", 24¾", 26¾"]

Yarn

Fingering weight yarn, 2 strands held together throughout. Per color you will need approx. 465yds/425m [525yds/480m, 601yds/550m, 684yds/625m, 766yds/700m, 848yds/775m, 930yds/850m, 1039yds/950m].

We used

2 [2, 3, 3, 3, 3, 4, 4] balls of Knitting For Olive Pure Silk Raspberry Pink – 100% silk

held together with...

2 [2, 3, 3, 3, 3, 4, 4] balls of Knitting for Olive Cotton Merino, Natural White - 70% organic cotton, 30% Merino wool (273yds/250m per 50g ball)
In the green sample, we have used Knitting For Olive, Merino in Clover Green and Knitting for Olive, Pure Silk in Ice Blue.
Alternative yarn suggestions: Gepard Garn Cotton Wool 3, Lana Grossa Cotton Wool, CaMaRose Økologisk Pimabomuld, Scheepjes Organicon

For a solid color version, use 1 strand of a heavy DK weight yarn, approx. 115yds/105m per 50g ball, or use half-balls of cotton leftovers as on page 14 for a striped version.

We used approx.

5 [5, 6, 6, 7, 8, 9, 9] skeins of Stylecraft Naturals Organic Cotton DK- 100% organic cotton (115yds/105m per 50g skein)
Alternative yarn suggestions: Gepard Garn Cotton Wool 5, Drops Cotton Merino, Rico Essentials Organic Cotton DK.

Recommended needles

US 7 (4.5mm) circular knitting needles, length 24-32in

Gauge

Stockinette stitch (blocked) on US 7 (4.5mm) needles 4 x 4in = 19.5 stitches x 26 rows

Stockinette stitch

Body

1. Cast on 126 [146, 166, 186, 206, 226, 246, 266] sts using the long tail cast on technique.

   Place a stitch marker to mark the start of the round and join to work in the round, being careful not to twist your sts.

2. K all sts.

3. Repeat step 2 until your piece measures 12in [12in, 11½in, 11½in, 11¼in, 11in, 10¾in, 10½in] from the cast-on edge (approx. 79 [78, 76, 76, 74, 72, 70, 68] more rounds).

4. Bind off 4 [4, 5, 6, 8, 10, 11, 12] sts, k59 [69, 78, 87, 95, 103, 112, 121] sts. Turn your work. You will now be working over these 59 [69, 78, 87, 95, 103, 112, 121] sts only to make the back of the top. (You will come back to the other sts later.)

5. Bind off 4 [4, 5, 6, 8, 10, 11, 12] sts, p55 [65, 73, 81, 87, 93, 101, 109]. Turn your work. (55 [65, 73, 81, 87, 93, 101, 109] sts.)

6. K1, ssk, k until 3 sts remain, k2tog, k1. (53 [63, 71, 79, 85, 91, 99, 107] sts.)

7. P1, p2tog, p until 3 sts remain, p2togtbl, p1. (51 [61, 69, 77, 83, 89, 97, 105] sts.)

8. Repeat steps 6 and 7 a further 2 [3, 4, 7, 8, 9, 11, 13] times. (43 [49, 53, 49, 51, 53, 53, 53] sts.)

9. K1, ssk, k until 3 sts remain, k2tog, k1. (41 [47, 51, 47, 49, 51, 51, 51] sts.)

10. P row.

11. Repeat steps 9 and 10 a further 3 [6, 8, 5, 5, 5, 4, 3] times. (35 [35, 35, 37, 39, 41, 43, 45] sts.)

12. K1, ssk, k until 3 sts remain, k2tog, k1. (33 [33, 33, 35, 37, 39, 41, 43] sts.)

13. Starting with a p row, work 3 rows in stockinette stitch.

14. Repeat steps 12 and 13 a further 3 [1, 0, 0, 0, 0, 0, 0] times. (27 [31, 33, 35, 37, 39, 41, 43] sts.)

Sizes 2, 3, 4, 5, 6, 7 and 8 only:

15. K1, ssk, k until 3 sts remain, k2tog, k1. ([29, 31, 33, 35, 37, 39, 41] sts.)

16. Starting with a p row, work in stockinette stitch until your piece measures 17in from the cast-on edge (approx. 1 more row). Make sure last row is a p row.

All sizes:

17. Now you will knit the top centre trim; this will look like reverse stockinette stitch on the RS of the top until it is folded and joined in the next step. Starting with a purl row, work in stockinette stitch until your trim measures 2½in (approx. 17 rows.) Make sure last row is a purl row.

18. Bind off using the folded bind off technique, folding the RS of the trim over to connect it to the first row of purl bumps on RS of top.

19. RS facing you, re-join yarn to 63 [73, 83, 93, 103, 113, 123, 133] sts waiting on your needle. Bind off 4 [4, 5, 6, 8, 10, 11, 12] sts, k until end of row. (59 [69, 78, 87, 95, 103, 112, 121] sts.)

20. Repeat steps 5 to 18 once more to make the front of your top, following only the steps for your size.

Straps

RS facing outwards, start at the underarm point of one of the armholes.

1. Working from right to left pick up and k 31 [32, 33, 33, 35, 36, 38, 39] sts until you reach the top of the trim on one side. Turn work so WS is facing you and use the cable cast on technique to cast on 27 [29, 31, 33, 35, 37, 39, 41] sts. (Note: If you want to make the straps longer, at this point you can cast on more sts.)

Strap cast on

Turn work back so the RS is facing you, making sure the cast-on sts are not twisted. Starting at the top of the trim on the adjoining side (where the arrow is pointing), pick up and k 31 [32, 33, 33, 35, 36, 38, 39] sts until you reach the point where you started. (89 [93, 97, 99, 105, 109, 115, 119 sts.)

Place a stitch marker to mark the start of the round and join to work in the round with the first st picked up.

2. P30 [31, 32, 32, 34, 35, 37, 38], p2tog, p25 [27, 29, 31, 33, 35, 37, 39], p2tog, p until you reach the marker. (87 [91, 95, 97, 103, 107, 113, 117] sts.)

3. Work every round in p until your trim measures 2½in (approx. 16 more rows).

4. Turn work as if to work back on the last sts of the round. Bind off using the folded bind off technique, folding the RS of the trim over to connect it to the first row of purl bumps on RS of top. Make sure you bind off loosely so the armhole is not too tight.

5. Repeat for the other side.

6. Weave in any loose ends.

We recommend that you block your top to achieve the correct measurements and keep the hem sitting flat.

Helix bag

For this pattern, we encourage you to create your own yarn through repurposing unwanted fabrics (see page 20). Knitted from the base up in twisted woven stitch, the Helix bag starts by knitting the base flat. Stitches are then picked up around the base and worked in the round to create the body of the bag. When the body is bound off, stitches are placed on a holder at either side of the bag. These stitches are knitted separately to form the handle, then seamed together at the top.

Size
One size

Flat measurements

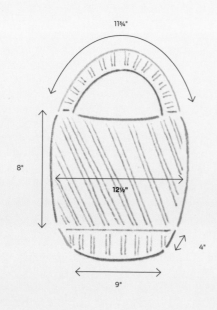

Yarn
Super bulky weight yarn, approx. 100yds/92m per 200g.

We repurposed fabric to use as yarn; you will need approx. 197yds to complete the bag. This is approx. one full-size sheet.

Recommended needles
US 19 (15mm) circular knitting needles, length 32in

Gauge
Twisted woven stitch (see page 41) unblocked:
4 x 4in = 6 stitches x 14 rows

Twisted woven stitch

Instructions

Base

1. Cast on 16 sts using the long tail cast on technique.

2. (WS) P all sts.

3. Repeat rows 1 and 2 of twisted woven stitch worked flat (see page 41) until the base measures 4in from the cast-on edge. Make sure last row worked is row 2.

4. Bind off 16 sts, leaving the final st on your needle; do not cut your yarn.

Body

1. RS facing outwards, working anti-clockwise from the st on your needle around the base of your bag, pick up and k 37 sts as follows: Pick up 5 sts along the shorter side until you reach the corner, pick up 14 sts along the cast-on edge, then another 5 sts along the second shorter side, then 13 sts until you reach the first st on your needle. (38 sts.) You will now be working in the round over these 38 sts. Place a stitch marker to mark the start of the round and continue working in the round.

2. K all sts.

3. Repeat rounds 1 and 2 of twisted woven stitch worked in the round (see page 41) until your bag measures 8in from where you picked up the sts in step 1 of the body. Make sure last round worked is round 2.

4. Cut the yarn, leaving a 6in yarn tail, and place the first 3 sts of the round on a st holder. Re-join yarn to sts waiting on needle and bind off 13sts. Cut and secure the yarn, then place the next 6 sts on a st holder. Re-join yarn to sts waiting on needle, then bind off 13 sts. Cut and secure the yarn, then place the last 3 sts on a st holder.

Note: At this point there should be 6 sts at each side of the bag to make the handles. Check these sts fall at the centre of each side. If you lost the yarn marker, you will need to adjust this step. To do so, lay the bag flat and place a marker on the top edge to mark the centre of each side of the bag, between 2 sts on the needle. Place 3 sts before and after the two markers on a st holder and bind off the rest.

Handle

1. RS facing outwards, slip 6 sts from one of the holders onto your needles, re-join yarn.

2. (RS) sl1k, *between the next 2 sts on the left needle, pick up and k 1 st from the row below, sl1pwyib*, repeat section in stars (*) until 1 st remains, k1. Turn work.

3. Sl1p, *p2tog*, repeat section in stars until 1 st remains, p1.

4. Repeat steps 2 and 3 until your handle measures 6in. Make sure last row worked is a RS row.

Note: 6in may seem short for half the handle, but we found that the handle stretched when the bag was worn. You can also adjust the handle length at this point if you would prefer a shorter or longer handle.

5. Bind off while repeating row 3, leaving a long yarn tail.

6. Re-join yarn to the 6 sts waiting on the other side of your bag. Repeat steps 2 to 5 once more.

7. RS facing outwards, work from left to right using the whip stitch technique to secure and join the handle bound-off edges together. Work each stitch twice to secure the handle.

8. Weave in all loose ends to neaten the front edges.

   Due to the nature of the fabric, we didn't block our Helix bag, but if you are using an alternative yarn you may wish to do so.

If you want to create more structure, you could try cutting the fabric into thicker strips or using a heavier material such as denim, going down a needle size.

Drift jacket

The Drift jacket combines an oversized cropped shape with chunky, irregular cables and an exaggerated ribbed neck. The jacket is worked flat in five pieces: the back, right front, left front, right sleeve and left sleeve. Each piece starts with a 1 x 1 rib and then changes to the irregular cable pattern. When the five pieces are complete, the front trims and shoulder seams are sewn together, then the 1 x 1 rib neck is picked up and knitted. Finally, the sleeves are sewn to the body and the buttons are attached.

Size

This pattern includes 8 sizes; see page 150 for size chart. Iris and Sana wear size 2. If you are in between sizes, we suggest going down a size as the jacket is designed with an oversized fit.

Flat measurements

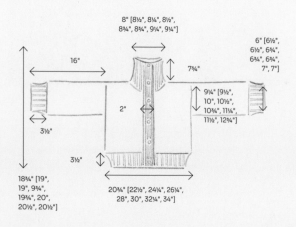

8" [8½", 8¼", 8½", 8¾", 8¾", 9¼", 9¼"]

16"

6" [6½", 6½", 6¾", 6¾", 6¾", 7", 7"]

7¾"

9¼" [9½", 10", 10½", 10¾", 11¼", 11½", 12¾"]

2"

3½"

3½"

18¾" [19", 19", 9¾", 19¾", 20", 20½", 20½"]

20¼" [22½", 24¼", 26¼", 28", 30", 32¼", 34"]

Yarn

Bulky weight yarn, approx. 110yds/100m per 100g.

We used

10 [10, 11, 12, 13, 14, 15, 16] balls of Wool and the Gang, Alpachino Merino in Tweed Gray – 60% Merino wool, 40% baby alpaca (110yds/100m per 100g ball)

In the yellow sample, we used Fonty Pole in color 404.

Alternative yarn suggestions: Drops Andes, Cascade Yarns 128

Extras

You will need 6 x 1in buttons.

Recommended needles

US 8 (5mm) knitting needles

(we suggest using circular knitting needles to work flat, length 24–32in)

US 11 (8mm) knitting needles and a cable needle

Gauge

Irregular cable (see page 43) on US 11 (8mm) needles:
4 x 4in = 16 stitches x 16 rows

1 x 1 rib stitch on US 8 (5mm) needles:
4 x 4in = 22 stitches x 22 rows

Irregular cable stitch

Instructions

Please refer to the charts available via the QR code on page 140 when referenced in the instructions.

Back

1. With US 8 (5mm) needles, cast on 61 [65, 71, 75, 81, 87, 93, 97] sts using the long tail cast on technique.

2. (WS) *p1, k1*, repeat section in stars (*) until 1 st remains, p1.

3. *K1, p1*, repeat section in stars until 1 st remains, k1.

4. Repeat steps 2 and 3 until your piece measures 3½in from the cast-on edge (approx. 17 more rows). Make sure last row worked is a WS row.

   Now change to US 11 (8mm) needles.

   Size 1 only:
5. (RS) P3, *k1, m1, k1, p1, m1p, p1, k1, m1, k2, m1, k1, p1, m1p, p1, k1, m1, k1, p1, m1p, p1*m repeat section in stars twice more. K1, m1, k1, p1, m1p, p1, k1, m1, k2, m1, k1, p1, m1p, p1, k3, p3. (87 sts.) Skip to step 16.

   Size 2 only:
6. (RS) P3, m1p, p1, *m1, k2, m1p, p2, m1, k2, m1, k2, m1p, p2, m1, k2, m1p, p3*, repeat section in stars a further 3 times, p1. (94 sts.) Skip to step 16.

   Size 3 only:
7. (RS) P3, m1p, *p1, m1, k2, m1p, p2, m1, k2, m1, k2, m1p, p2, m1, k2, m1p, p4*, repeat section in stars a further 3 times. (100 sts.)

8. K5, *p3, k3, p6, k3, p3, k6*, repeat section in stars twice more. P3, k3, p6, k3, p3, k5.

9. P5, *k3, p3, k6, p3, k3, p6*, repeat section in stars twice more. K3, p3, k6, p3, k3, p5.

10. Repeat step 8 once more. Skip to step 19.

   Size 4 only:
11. (RS) P3, k3, *m1p, p2, m1, k2, m1, k2, m1p, p2, m1, k2, m1p, p2, m1, k2*, repeat section in stars a further 3 times. M1p, p2, m1, k2, m1, k2, m1p, p2, m1, k2, p3. (108 sts.) Skip to step 16.

   Size 5 only:
12. (RS) P5, *m1, k2, m1p, p2, m1, k2, m1, k2, m1p, p2, m1, k2, m1p, p3*, repeat section in stars a further 4 times, p1. (116 sts.) Skip to step 16.

   Size 6 only:
13. (RS) p2, m1p, p4, *m1, k2, m1p, p2, m1, k2, m1, k2, m1p, p2, m1, k2, m1p, p4*, repeat section in stars a further 4 times, m1p, p1. (124 sts.) Skip to step 16.

   Size 7 only:
14. (RS) P5, *m1, k2, m1p, p2, m1, k2, m1, k2, m1p, p2, m1, k2, m1p, p2*, repeat section in stars a further 4 times. M1, k2, m1p, p2, m1, k2, m1, k2, m1p, p2, k3, p5. (133 sts.) Skip to step 16.

   Size 8 only:
15. (RS) P2, m1p, p3, *m1, k2, m1p, p2, m1, k2, m1, k2, m1p, p2, m1, k2, m1p, p3*, repeat section in stars a further 5 times, p2. (140 sts.)

Sizes 1, 2, 4, 5, 6, 7 and 8 only:

16. (WS) K0 [k1, k0, k1, k2, k2, k2], *k3 [k4, k3, k4, k5, k3, k4], p3, k3, p6, k3, p3*, repeat section in stars a further 3 [3, 4, 4, 4, 5, 5] times, k3 [k5, k3, k5, k7, k5, k6].

17. P0 [p1, p0, p1, p2, p2, p2], *p3 [p4, p3, p4, p5, p3, p4], k3, p3, k6, p3, k3*, repeat section in stars a further 3 [3, 4, 4, 4, 5, 5] times, p3 [p5, p3, p5, p7, p5, p6].

18. Repeat step 16 once more.

All sizes:

19. Starting with row 1 (RS row), follow the back chart until you finish row 36 of the chart (see QR code on page 140). Make sure you follow the correct chart for your size.

20. Repeat rows 1 to 16 [18, 18, 20, 20, 22, 24, 24] of the back chart.

21. Starting with row 1 (RS row), follow the right back neck chart until you finish row 6 of the chart. (57 [63, 69, 75, 83, 91, 99, 105] sts in two sections.)

22. Bind off 28 [31, 34, 37, 41, 45, 49, 52] sts.

23. RS facing outwards, re-join yarn to 29 [32, 35, 38, 42, 46, 50, 53] sts waiting on the needle. Starting with row 1 (RS row), follow the left back neck chart until you finish row 2 of the chart.

24. Bind off 28 [31, 34, 37, 41, 45, 49, 52] sts.

Right front

1. With US 8 (5mm) needles, cast on 42 [44, 46, 50, 52, 56, 58, 60] sts using the long tail cast on technique.

2. (WS) Sl1p *k1, p1*, repeat section in stars until 1 st remains, k1.

3. *P1, k1*, repeat section in stars until end of row.

4. Repeat steps 2 and 3 until your piece measures 3½in from the cast-on edge (approx. 17 more rows). Make sure last row worked is a WS row.

Now change to US 11 (8mm) needles.

Size 1 only:

5. (RS) P1, *m1, k2, m1p, p2, m1, k2, m1, k2, m1p, p2, m1, k2*, m1p, p2, repeat section in stars once more, k1. Slip the last 14 sts onto a st holder or scrap piece of yarn. Turn work. (41 sts.)

6. P4, *k3, p6, k3, p3*, k3, p3, repeat section in stars once more, k1.

7. P1, *k3, p3, k6, p3, k3*, p3, repeat section in stars once more, k1.

8. Repeat step 6 once more. Skip to step 22.

Size 2 only:

9. (RS) P1, *m1, k2, m1p, p2, m1, k2, m1, k2, m1p, p2, m1, k2, m1p, p2*, repeat section in stars once more, p1. Slip the last 14 sts onto a st holder or scrap piece of yarn. Turn work. (44 sts.) Skip to step 19.

Size 3 only:
10. (RS) P1, *m1p, p2, m1, k2, m1p, p2, m1, k2, m1, k2, m1p, p2, m1, k2*, repeat section in stars once more, m1p, p3. Slip the last 14 sts onto a st holder or scrap piece of yarn. Turn work. (47 sts.) Skip to step 19.

Size 4 only:
11. (RS) P1, *p2, m1p, p2, m1, k2, m1p, p2, m1, k2, m1, k2, m1p, p2, m1, k2*, repeat section in stars once more, m1p, p3. Slip the last 14 sts onto a st holder or scrap piece of yarn. Turn work. (51 sts.) Skip to step 19.

Size 5 only:
12. (RS) P1, *m1p, p3, m1p, p2, m1, k2, m1p, p2, m1, k2, m1, k2, m1p, p2, m1, k2*, repeat section in stars once more, m1p, p3. Slip the last 14 sts onto a st holder or scrap piece of yarn. Turn work. (55 sts.) Skip to step 19.

Size 6 only:
13. (RS) P1, *m1, k2, m1p, p2, m1, k2, m1, k2, m1p, p2, m1, k2, p2*, repeat section in stars once more, m1, k2, m1p, p2, m1, k2, m1, k2, m1p, p2, m1, k3. Slip the last 14 sts onto a st holder or scrap piece of yarn. Turn work. (60 sts.)

14. P4, *k3, p6, k3, p3, k2, p3*, repeat section in stars once more, k3, p6, k3, p3, k1.

15. P1, k3, *p3, k6, p3, k3, p2, k3*, repeat section in stars once more, p3, k6, p3, k4.

16. Repeat step 14 once more. Skip to step 22.

Size 7 only:
17. (RS) P1, *m1, k2, m1p, p2, m1, k2, m1, k2, m1p, p2, m1, k2, m1p, p2*, repeat section in stars once more, m1, k2, m1p, p2, m1, k2, m1, k2, m1p, p2, m1, k2, p3. Slip the last 14 sts onto a st holder or scrap piece of yarn.

Turn work. (64 sts.) Skip to step 19.

Size 8 only:
18. (RS) P1, *m1, k2, m1p, p2, m1, k2, m1, k2, m1p, p2, m1, k2, m1p, p3*, repeat section in stars once more, m1, k2, m1p, p2, m1, k2, m1, k2, m1p, p2, m1, k2, m1p, p2, m1p, p1. Slip the last 14 sts onto a st holder or scrap piece of yarn. Turn work. (68 sts.)

Sizes 2, 3, 4, 5, 7 and 8 only:
19. (WS) [K1, k1, k1, k1, k0, k2], *k3, p3, k3, p6, k3, p3, [k0, k0, k2, k4, k0, k1]*, repeat section in stars a further [1, 1, 1, 1, 2, 2] times, [k1, k4, k4, k4, k1, k0].

20. [P1, p4, p6, p8, p1, p1], *k3, p3, k6, p3, k3, [p3, p3, p3, p3, p3, p4]*, [p0, p0, p2, p4, p0, p0], repeat section in stars a further [1, 1, 1, 1, 2, 2] times, [p1, p1, p1, p1, p0, p1].

21. Repeat step 19 once more.

All sizes:
22. Starting with row 1 (RS row), follow the right front chart until you finish row 58 [60, 60, 62, 62, 64, 66, 66] of the chart.

23. Bind off.

24. RS facing outwards, slip the 14 sts held on the st holder onto US 8 (5mm) needles, slipping the sts from right to left onto the needle.

25. (RS) Re-join yarn to the 14 sts. *P1, k1*, repeat section in stars until end of row.

26. Sl1p *k1, p1*, repeat section in stars until 1 st remains, k1.

27. Repeat steps 25 and 26 until your piece measures 15in [15½in, 15½in, 16in, 16in,

15½in, 16in, 16in] from cast on edge (approx. 64 [66, 66, 68, 68, 66, 68, 68] more rows. 85 [87, 87, 89, 89, 87, 89, 89] rows in total including hem). Make sure last row worked is a WS row.

28. Instead of binding off, place sts on a st holder or scrap piece of yarn.

Left front

1. With US 8 (5mm) needles, cast on 42 [44, 46, 50, 52, 56, 58, 60] sts using the long tail cast on technique.

2. (WS) *K1, p1*, repeat section in stars until end of row.

3. Sl1k, *p1, k1*, repeat section in stars until 1 st remains, p1.

4. Repeat step 2 once more.

5. Sl1k, p1, k1, p1, k1, p1, k1, turn your work. You will now be working across these 7 sts only to form the first buttonhole. (You will come back to the other sts later.)

6. Sl1p, k1, p1, k1, p1, k1, p1.

7. Sl1k, p1, k1, p1, k1, p1, k1.

8. Repeat steps 6 and 7 once more. Cut your yarn leaving 6in yarn tail.

9. RS facing outwards, re-join yarn to the 35 [37, 39, 43, 45, 49, 51, 53] sts on your needle. (You will now be working across these sts only.)

10. Sl1p, *k1, p1*, repeat section in stars until end of row.

11. *K1, p1*, repeat section in stars until 1 st remains, k1.

12. Repeat steps 10 and 11 once more.

13. Repeat step 10 once more.

14. Working back across all 42 [44, 46, 50, 52, 56, 58, 60] sts on your needle, repeat steps 2 and 3 until your piece measures 3½in from the cast-on edge (approx. 11 more rows). Make sure the last row worked is a WS row.

15. Cut your yarn leaving 6in yarn tail and slip the first 14 sts onto a st holder or scrap piece of yarn. RS facing outwards, re-join yarn to 28 [30, 32, 36, 38, 42, 44, 46] sts on needle.

Now change to US 11 (8mm) needles.

Size 1 only:
16. K1, *k2, m1, p2, m1p, k2, m1, k2, m1, p2, m1p, k2, m1*, p2, m1p, repeat section in stars once more, p1. (41 sts)

17. K1, *p3, k3, p6, k3, p3*, k3, repeat section in stars once more, p1.

18. K1, *k3, p3, k6, p3, k3*, p3, repeat section in stars once more, p1.

19. Repeat step 17 once more. Skip to step 36.

Size 2 only:
20. P1, *m1p, p2, m1, k2, m1p, p2, m1, k2, m1, k2, m1p, p2, m1, k2*, repeat section in stars once more, p1. (44 sts.) Skip to step 30.

Size 3 only:

21. P1, *m1p, p2, m1, k2, m1p, p2, m1, k2, m1, k2, m1p, p2, m1, k2*, repeat section in stars once more, m1p, p3. (47 sts.) Skip to step 30.

Size 4 only:

22. P2, m1p, p1, *m1, k2, m1p, p2, m1, k2, m1, k2, m1p, p2, m1, k2, m1p, p4*, repeat section in stars once more, p1. (51 sts.) Skip to step 30.

Size 5 only:

23. P2, m1p, p1, *m1, k2, m1p, p2, m1, k2, m1, k2, m1p, p2, m1, k2, m1p, p2, m1p, p3*, repeat section in stars once more, p1. (55 sts.) Skip to step 30.

Size 6 only:

24. K1, *m1, k2, m1p, p2, m1, k2, m1, k2, m1p, p2, m1, k2, p2*, repeat section in stars once more. M1, k2, m1p, p2, m1, k2, m1, k2, m1p, p2, m1, k2, p1. (60 sts.)

25. K1, *p3, k3, p6, k3, p3, k2*, repeat section in stars once more, p3, k3, p6, k3, p4.

26. K1, *k3, p3, k6, p3, k3, p2* repeat section in stars once more, k3, p3, k6, p3, k3, p1.

27. Repeat step 25 once more. Skip to step 36.

Size 7 only:

28. *P2, m1p, k2, m1, p2, m1p, k2, m1, k2, m1, p2, m1p, k2, m1*, repeat section in stars once more. P3, m1, k2, m1p, p2, m1, k2, m1, k2, m1p, p2, m1, k2, p1 (64 sts.) Skip to step 33.

Size 8 only:

29. P1, m1p, *p2, m1p, k2, m1, p2, m1p, k2, m1, k2, m1, p2, m1p, k2, m1, p1*, repeat section in stars twice more. (68 sts.) Skip to step 33.

Sizes 2, 3, 4, and 5 only:

30. [K1, k4, k6, k8], *p3, k3, p6, k3, p3*, [k3, k3, k5, k7], repeat section in stars once more, k4.

31. P1, *p3, k3, p3, k6, p3, k3*, [p0, p0, p2, p4], repeat section in stars once more, [p1, p4, p6, p8].

32. Repeat step 30 once more. Skip to step 36.

Sizes 7 and 8 only:

33. K1, *p3, k3, p6, k3, p3, [k3, k4]*, repeat section in stars twice more, [k0, k1].

34. [P0, p1], *[p3, p4], k3, p3, k6, p3, k3*, repeat section in stars twice more, p1.

35. Repeat step 33 once more.

All sizes:

36. Starting with row 1 (RS row), follow the left front chart until you finish row 58 [60, 60, 62, 62, 64, 66, 66] of the chart.

37. Bind off.

38. RS facing outwards, slip the 14 sts held on the left front st holder onto US 8 (5mm) needles, slipping the sts from right to left onto the needle. Re-join yarn to 14 sts.

39. (RS) Sl1k, *p1, k1*, repeat section in stars until 1 st remains, p1.

40. *K1, p1*, repeat section in stars until end of row.

41. Repeat steps 39 and 40 a further 3 times (6 more rows).

42. Sl1k, p1, k1, p1, k1, p1, k1, turn your work. You will now be working across these 7 sts only. (You will come back to the other sts later.)

43. Sl1p, k1, p1, k1, p1, k1, p1.

44. Sl1k, p1, k1, p1, k1, p1, k1.

45. Repeat steps 43 and 44 once more. Cut your yarn leaving 6in yarn tail.

46. RS facing outwards, re-join yarn to the 7 sts on your left needle. (You will now be working across these 7 sts only.)

47. Sl1p, k1, p1, k1, p1, k1, p1.

48. K1, p1, k1, p1, k1, p1, k1.

49. Repeat steps 47 and 48 once more.

50. Repeat step 47 once more.

51. Working back across all 14 sts on your needle, (WS) *k1, p1*, repeat section in stars until end of row.

52. Sl1k, *p1, k1*, repeat section in stars until 1 st remains, p1.

53. Repeat steps 51 and 52 until your piece measures 3½in from the top of the last buttonhole (17 more rows). Make sure last row worked is a WS row.

54. Repeat steps 42 to 53 once more.

55. Repeat steps 42 to 50 once more.

56. Repeat steps 51 and 52 until your piece measures 1in [1¼in, 1¼in, 1½in, 1½in, 1¼in, 1½in, 1½in] from the top of the last buttonhole (5 [7, 7, 9, 9, 7, 9, 9] more rows). Make sure last row worked is a WS row.

57. Place 14 sts onto a st holder or scrap piece of yarn.

Right Sleeve

1. With US 8 (5mm) needles, cast on 58 [60, 60, 62, 62, 62, 64, 64] sts using the long tail cast on technique.

2. (WS) *K1, p1*, repeat section in stars until end of row.

3. Repeat step 2 until your piece measures 3½in (approx. 18 more rows). Make sure last row worked is a WS row.

   Now change to US 11 (8mm) needles.

Sizes 1 and 2 only:

4. (RS) P7 [p8], m1p, p1, *k2, m1, p2, m1p, k2, m1, k2, m1, p2, m1p, k2, m1, p3*, repeat section in stars twice more, m1p, p5 [p6]. (78 [80] sts.) Skip to step 9.

Sizes 3 and 4 only:

5. (RS) [P5, p8] *m1p, [p2, p1], m1p, p1, m1, k2, m1p, p2, m1, k2, m1, k2, m1p, p2, m1, k2*, repeat section in stars twice more, [p10, p12]. ([84, 86] sts.) Skip to step 9.

Size 5 only:

6. (RS) P3, m1p, p2 *m1p, p2, m1p, p2, m1, k2, m1p, p2, m1, k2, m1, k2, m1p, p2, m1, k2*, repeat section in stars (*) twice more, m1p, p2, m1p, p2, m1p, p5. (90 sts.) Skip to step 9.

Sizes 6 and 7 only:

7. (RS) [P2, p3], m1p, *p2, m1p, k2, m1, p2, m1p, k2, m1, k2, m1, p2, m1p, k2, m1*, repeat section in stars a further 3 times, p1, m1p, p1, m1p, [p2, p3]. ([93, 95] sts.) Skip to step 9.

Size 8 only:

8. (RS) P2, *p1, m1p, p2, m1, k2, m1p, p2, m1, k2, m1, k2, m1p, p2, m1, k1, m1*, repeat section in stars a further 3 times, p6. (96 sts.)

All sizes:

9. K9 [k10, k10, k12, k12, k6, k7, k6], *p3, k3, p6, k3, p3, k3 [k3, k5, k4, k6, k3, k3, k4]*, repeat section in stars a further [2, 2, 2, 2, 2, 3, 3, 3] times, k6 [k7, k5, k8, k6, k3, k4, k2].

10. P9 [p10, p10, p12, p12, p6, p7, p6], *k3, p3, k6, p3, k3, p3 [p3, p5, p4, p6, p3, p3, p4]*, repeat section in stars a further [2, 2, 2, 2, 2, 3, 3, 3] times, p6 [p7, p5, p8, p6, p3, p4, p2].

11. Repeat step 9 once more.

12. Starting with row 1 (RS row), follow the right sleeve chart until you finish row 36 of the chart.

13. Repeat rows 1 to 12 of the right sleeve chart.

14. Bind off. It's useful to attach a marker to your sleeve at this point to remember which is the right sleeve.

Left sleeve

1. Repeat steps 1 to 11 as for the right sleeve, only working the steps for your size.

2. Starting with row 1 (RS row), follow the left sleeve chart until you finish row 36 of the chart.

3. Repeat row 1 to 12 of the left sleeve chart.

4. Bind off.

Front trim seams

The front rib trims need to be joined to the fronts of the cardigan. RS facing outwards, use the vertical invisible seam technique to sew the left trim to the left front and the right trim to the right front. Start from the top of the hem and work upwards until you reach the sts waiting on the st holders.

Shoulder seams

RS facing outwards, place the front pieces on top of the back. Starting from the outside edges, use the horizontal invisible seam technique to sew the shoulder seams together.

Neck 1 x 1 rib

1. RS facing outwards, slip the 14 sts held on the left front st holder onto US 8 (5mm) needles, slipping the sts from left to right onto the needle. Re-join yarn and pick up 18 [18, 18, 20, 20, 20, 22, 22] sts along the left front neckline until you reach the shoulder seam, then pick up 37 [39, 39, 41, 41, 41, 41, 43] sts along the back neck until you reach the other shoulder seam. Pick up 18 [18, 18, 20, 20, 20, 22, 22] sts along the right front until you reach the 14 sts on the right front st holder. Cut your yarn leaving 6in tail, then slip the 14 sts onto your needle, from left to right. Turn work and re-join yarn. (101 [103, 103, 109, 109, 109, 113, 115] sts.)

2. (WS) Sl1p, *k1, p1*, repeat section in stars until end of row.

3. Sl1k, *p1, k1*, repeat section in stars until end of row

4. Repeat steps 2 and 3 until rib measures 2¼in [2in, 2in, 2in, 2in, 2in, 2in, 2in] from picking up the sts in step 1 (approx. 11 [9, 9, 9, 9, 9, 9, 9] more rows). Make sure last row worked is a WS row.

5. Sl1k, p1, k1, p1, k1, p1, k1, turn your work. You will now be working across these 7 sts only. (You will come back to the other sts later.)

6. Sl1p, k1, p1, k1, p1, k1, p1.

7. Sl1k, p1, k1, p1, k1, p1, k1.

8. Repeat steps 6 and 7 once more. Cut your yarn leaving 6in yarn tail.

9. RS facing outwards, re-join yarn to the sts on your left needle. You will now be working across these 94 [96, 96, 102, 102, 102, 106, 108] sts only.

10. Sl1p, *k1, p1*, repeat section in stars until 1 st remains, k1.

11. Repeat step 10 a further 4 times.

12. Working back across all 101 [103, 103, 109, 109, 109, 113, 115] sts on your needle, repeat steps 2 and 3 until your piece measures 3in [3½in, 3½in, 3½in, 3½in, 3½in, 3½in, 3½in] from the top of the last buttonhole (approx. 17 [19, 19, 19, 19, 19, 19, 19] rows). Make sure last row is a WS row.

13. Repeat steps 5 to 11 once more.

14. Working back across all sts on your needle, Repeat steps 2 and 3 once more (2 more rows).

15. Repeat step 2 once more.

16. Bind off in ribbing

Armhole seams

RS facing outwards, use a stitch marker or short piece of yarn to mark the centre of the right sleeve and match this with the right shoulder seam. Measure 9¾in [10in, 10½in, 10¾in, 11¼in, 11½in, 12in, 12½in] down the sides of the front and back and place markers. Match these to the outer edges of the sleeve. Use the perpendicular invisible seam technique to sew the right sleeve to the right side of the body. Repeat to join the left sleeve to the left side of the body.

Side seams and sleeve seams

RS facing outwards, starting at the hem, use the vertical invisible seam technique to sew the sides of the front and back together, then continue and sew the sleeve seams together in the same way. Weave in any loose ends.

Depending on what yarn you are using, you may want to block your jacket to achieve the correct measurements.

Buttons

Place front left trim on top of right trim and mark where buttonholes need to be, or sew buttons to the centre of the front right trim as follows:

Sew button 1 so the centre sits 1in [1¾in, 1¾in, 1¾in, 1¾in, 1¾in, 1¾in, 1¾in] from the cast-on hem.

Sew button 2 so the centre sits 4¼in from the centre of button 1.

Sew button 3 so the centre sits 4¼in from the centre of button 2.

Sew button 4 so the centre sits 4¼in from the centre of button 3.

Sew button 5 so the centre sits 4in [4in, 4in, 4½in, 4½in, 4in, 4½in, 4½in] from the centre of button 4.

Sew button 6 so the centre sits 4in [4¼in, 4¼in, 4¼in, 4¼in, 4¼in, 4¼in, 4¼in] from the centre of button 5.

QR code

Check out the hashtag #driftjacket to see all the different colors made by the community.

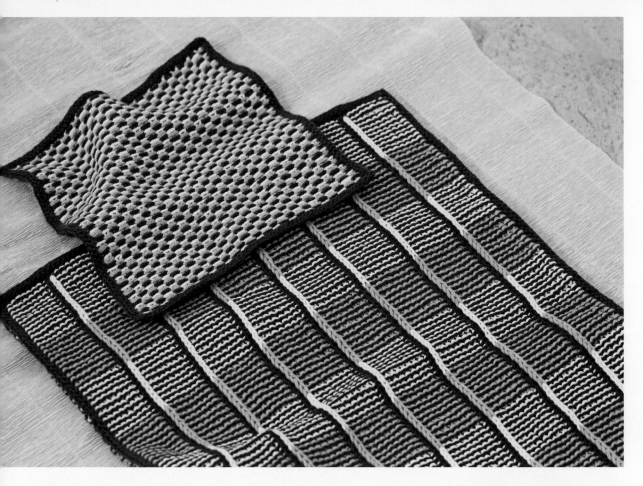

Garter stripe and double linen stitch

Knit

Anni cloth set

The Anni cloth set explores vibrant three-color stitches in practical kitchen textiles. The set is made up of a tea towel knitted using garter stripe stitch and a cloth knitted in double linen stitch. Both pieces feature a picked-up knitted edging.

Flat measurements

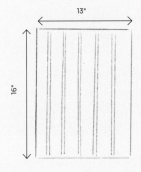

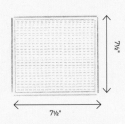

Yarn

DK/Sport weight yarn in three colors.
We recommend using a hardwearing cotton yarn. For the tea towel, you will need approx. 180yds/165m of color A, 91yds/83m of color B, and 58yds/53m of color C. For the cloth, you will need approx. 55yds/50m of color A, 36yds/33m of color B and 34yds/31m of color C.

We used

Color A – Dark green
2 balls of Krea Deluxe Organic Cotton in color 45 – 100% organic cotton (180yds/165m per 50g ball)

Color B – White
1 ball of Krea Deluxe Organic Cotton in color 01 – 100% organic cotton (180yds/165m per 50g ball)

Color C – Blue
1 ball of Stylecraft Naturals Organic Cotton in color 7198 Azure – 100% organic cotton (115yds/105m per 50g ball)

Alternative yarn suggestions: Quince & Co Willet, Drops Safran, Cascade Yarns Ultra Pima

Recommended needles

US 4 (3.5mm) circular knitting needles, length 16–20 to work flat.

Gauge

Garter stripe stitch (see page 44) after blocking: 4 x 4in = 24 stitches x 47 rows

Double linen stitch (see page 45) after blocking: 4 x 4in = 30 stitches x 68 rows

Knitting notes

- For the tea towel, two colors alternate every row. To avoid cutting yarns after each row, we suggest using circular needles to work flat. When the next color to be worked is on the opposite side of the needle, the pattern will instruct you to slide your stitches to the other side of your circular needle, so that the correct color is ready to start the next row.

- For the neatest finish, bind off the edging tightly.

Instructions

Tea towel

1. With color A, cast on 80 sts using the cable cast on technique.

2. (RS) K all sts. Turn work.

3. (WS) With color B, k9, *p1, sl1p, k8*, repeat section in stars (*) until 1 st remains, k1. Slide sts to the other end of the needles.

4. (WS) With color A, p9, *sl1p, p9*, repeat section in stars until 1 st remains, p1. Turn work.

5. (RS) With color B, p9, *sl1pwyib, k1, p8*, repeat section in stars until 1 st remains, p1. Slide sts to the other end of the needles.

6. (RS) With color A, k10, *sl1pwyib, k9*, repeat section in stars until end of row. Turn work.

7. Repeat steps 3 to 6 a further 5 times. (20 rows.)

8. With colors A and C, repeat steps 3 to 6 a further 5 times. When color B is mentioned, replace with color C. (20 rows.)

9. With colors A and B, repeat steps 3 to 6 a further 5 times. (20 rows.)

10. Repeat steps 8 and 9 a further 3 times. (120 rows.)

11. With colors A and B, repeat steps 3 to 5 once more. (3 rows.) Cut color B.

12. With color A, starting with a RS row, k 2 rows.

13. Bind off, leaving the last st on the needle to start the edging in the next step.

14. Rotate piece 90 degrees clockwise, so the left longer side now sits at the top. Pick up and k 97 sts, picking up the stitches on the flat rows of the garter pattern, between each ridged row. (98 sts.)

15. K until 2 sts remain, k2tog. (97 sts.)

16. Bind off, leaving the last st on the needle to start the next step.

17. Rotate piece 90 degrees clockwise, so the cast-on edge now sits at the top. Pick up and k 81 sts. (82 sts.)

18. Repeat steps 15 and 16 once more.

19. Rotate piece 90 degrees clockwise, so the right longer side now sits at the top. Pick up and k 98 sts. (99 sts.)

20. Sl1p, k until 2 sts remain, k2tog. (98 sts.)

21. Bind off and weave in ends. We recommend blocking the tea towel.

To add a loop for hanging the finished pieces:
Cast on 15 sts using the long tail cast on technique, k1 row, then bind off. Sew each end to one of the WS top corners.

Cloth

1. With color A, cast on 56 sts using the long tail cast on technique.

2. (WS) With color A, p all sts.

3. Work rows 1 and 2 of double linen stitch (see page 45) until your cloth measures 7in. Make sure last row worked is row 2 using color A.

4. (RS) With color A, k 2 rows.

5. Bind off, leaving the last st on the needle to start the next step.

6. Rotate piece 90 degrees clockwise, so the left edge now sits at the top. Pick up and k 58 sts. (59 sts.)

7. Repeat steps 15 and 16 of the tea towel once.

8. Rotate piece 90 degrees clockwise, so the cast-on edge now sits at the top. Pick up and k 58 sts. (59 sts.)

9. Repeat steps 15 and 16 of the tea towel once.

10. Rotate piece 90 degrees clockwise, so the right edge now sits at the top. Pick up and k 60 sts. (61 sts.)

11. Sl1p, k until 2 sts remain, k2tog. (60 sts.)

12. Bind off and weave in ends. We recommend blocking the cloth.

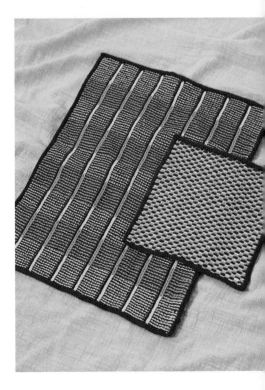

Good
to know

Notes about our patterns

All left and right instructions are written as if you are looking at your knitting.

Check for knitting notes in the information at the start of each pattern. These contain key information specific to each pattern.

Unless stated otherwise in the pattern knitting notes, when binding off in the middle of a row, 1 stitch remains on the right needle. This is included in the instructions after the bind off. For example: '**Bind off 15 sts, p2**'. The p2 includes the 1 stitch on the right needle.

If the pattern instructs you to bind off in ribbing, bind off in the rib pattern you have been working in.

When instructed to place a stitch marker to mark the start of the round, continue moving it up with every round you work.

We recommend doing a gauge swatch before you start, to make sure you get the best possible outcome. The suggested needle size is provided at the start of each pattern, but based on your gauge, you may wish to go up or down a size.

We suggest the type of needles for each pattern. In cases where multiple circular needles are required, you can also use the larger length needle and the magic loop method when a smaller length is needed.

Useful tools to have: tape measure, stitch markers, stitch holders, small sharp scissors, blunt tapestry needle to seam and weave in ends, a sharp sewing needle to sew on buttons, blocking mats and pins.

Sizing

For the garments in this book, please use the chart below to select your size. Unless stated otherwise, when the instructions differ between sizes, they will be written as follows: **size 1 [size 2, size 3, size 4, size 5, size 6, size 7, size 8].**

Size	To fit chest
1	28-30"
2	32-34"
3	36-38"
4	40-42"
5	44-46"
6	48-50"
7	52-54"
8	56-58"

The best way to find your size is to measure the widest part of your chest and select the closest corresponding size. If you are in between sizes, refer to any sizing notes provided in the pattern or size up for a more oversized look and size down for a more fitted garment. If you are still unsure which size to pick, use the flat measurements provided in the patterns as a guide. Measure a similar garment that you like the fit of and compare its measurements to find the closest size match.

Abbreviations

To make our patterns more concise and easier to read, knitting abbreviations are used to shorten knitting terms. Here's a list of all abbreviations and meanings:

k – knit.

p – purl.

st(s) – stitch(es).

WS – wrong side.

RS – right side.

dpns – double pointed needles

a – color A, used after other abbreviations in the Static mittens pattern to show that you work the stitch or technique in color A.

b – color B, used after other abbreviations in the Static mittens pattern to show that you work the stitch or technique in color B.

yf – bring yarn(s) to front of work.

yb – take yarn(s) to back of work.

sl – slip.

sl1k – slip 1 stitch knitwise with yarn at back.

sl1p – slip 1 stitch purlwise with yarn at front. Refer to the number after sl for how many stitches to slip.

sl1pwyib – slip 1 stitch purlwise with yarn at back. Refer to the number after sl for how many stitches to slip.

ssk – decrease 1 stitch by slipping the next two stitches knitwise, one by one. Insert the left needle through the front loops of both slipped stitches and knit them together to make 1 stitch.

k2tog – decrease 1 stitch by knitting 2 stitches together.

k2togtbl – decrease 1 stitch by knitting 2 stitches together through the back loop.

p2tog – decrease 1 stitch by purling 2 stitches together.

p2togtbl – decrease 1 stitch by inserting the right needle purlwise into the next 2 stitches on the left needle through the back loops, starting with the stitch furthest away. Purl together to make 1 stitch.

CDD – central double decrease, decreases 2 stitches at the same time knitwise. Slip 2 stitches together knitwise, knit the next stitch, then slip the two slipped stitches over the knit stitch.

CDDP – central double decrease purlwise, decreases 2 stitches at the same time purlwise. Slip the next 2 stitches knitwise, one by one. Insert the left needle from right to left through the first slipped stitch and then the second slipped stitch, slipping them back to the left needle while reversing the order. Purl 3 stitches together to make 1 stitch.

m1 and m1L – make 1 stitch left leaning. Pick up the horizontal strand before the next stitch from front to back and knit into the back of it.

m1R – make 1 stitch right leaning. Pick up the horizontal strand before the next stitch from back to front and knit into the front of it.

m1p – make 1 stitch purlwise. Pick up the horizontal strand before the next stitch from the front to back and purl into the back of it.

k1fb – Increase 1 stitch by knitting into the front and back of the stitch.

CDI(aba) – central double increase creates 3 stitches from 1 stitch. Alternate yarn when working this technique for the Static mittens. Use color A to knit into the back of the next stitch, then color B to knit into the front of the same stitch. Identify the strand between the two stitches just created, lift it onto the left needle and use color A to knit into the back of it. Make sure you pull the yarns tight.

sk – skip

sk3, p3 over, p3 – skip 3 stitches, purl 3 over skipped stitches, purl 3 skipped stitches (see page 33).

Loop1L – loop 1 left (see page 29).

Loop1R – loop 1 right (see page 30).

r – rectangle

Charts

Some of the patterns in this book use charts to simplify steps when instructions differ between sizes, often when increasing and decreasing are involved. A few things to know about our charts:

Each chart is made up of squares,
each square represents one stitch.

The symbols in each square
represent the way the stitch is worked, referenced in the key below.

The color filled in each square
represents the yarn color, this is referenced in the color key when working with more than one color.

The first row/round in all charts
is the bottom row/round.

The number at each side of the chart
indicates the row/round number as well as the direction of reading.

Right side rows are read from right to left and **wrong side rows** are read from left to right.

Rounds are read from right to left.

Charts show work as it appears, with the right side facing.

Red line highlights a section that needs to be repeated.

Chart key

☐	**No symbol** = **RS:** knit; **WS:** purl
▣	**RS:** purl; **WS:** knit
V	**RS:** slip 1 stitch purlwise with yarn at back **WS:** slip 1 stitch purlwise with yarn at front
V̲	**RS:** slip 1 stitch purlwise with yarn at front **WS:** slip 1 stitch purlwise with yarn at back
◿	**RS:** k2tog; **WS:** p2tog

$\boxed{\diagdown}$	**RS:** ssk; **WS:** p2togtbl
$\boxed{\text{L}}$	Make 1 stitch left leaning
$\boxed{\text{R}}$	Make 1 stitch right leaning
$\boxed{\cap}$	Loop 1 left
$\boxed{\cap}$	Loop 1 right
	Slip the next 3 sts onto cable needle and hold at front of work, k1 from left-hand needle, then k3 from cable needle
	Slip the next st onto cable needle and hold at back of work, k3 from left-hand needle, then k1 from cable needle
	Slip the next 3 sts onto cable needle and hold at front of work, p1 from left-hand needle, then k3 from cable needle
	Slip the next st onto cable needle and hold at back of work, k3 from left-hand needle, then p1 from cable needle
	Slip the next 3 sts onto cable needle and hold at front of work, k2 from left-hand needle, then k3 from cable needle
	Slip the next 2 sts onto cable needle and hold at back of work, k3 from left-hand needle, then k2 from cable needle
	Slip the next 3 sts onto cable needle and hold at front of work, p2 from left-hand needle, then k3 from cable needle
	Slip the next 2 sts onto cable needle and hold at back of work, k3 from left-hand needle, then p2 from cable needle
	Slip the next 3 sts onto cable needle and hold at front of work, k3 from left-hand needle, then k3 from cable needle
	Slip the next 3 sts onto cable needle and hold at back of work, k3 from left-hand needle, then k3 from cable needle

Upstream sweater charts

The bold black line shows where the marker is. Slip the markers after m1R as you have been doing. Work the raglan increases and the following sts, then repeat the section in red until you reach the next marker. Unless stated otherwise, start the chart row again, repeating this process to work the chart across the front, left sleeve, back and right sleeve until you reach marker 1 where you started.

Size 1 and 2 raglan

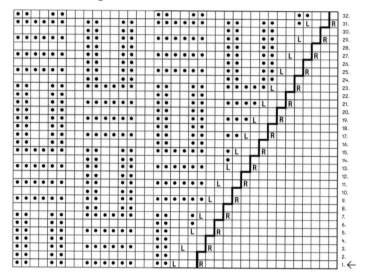

Size 3 raglan

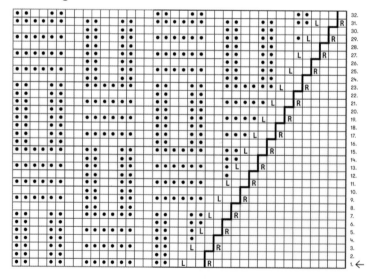

Sizes 4–8 have separate sleeve and front/back charts; this is because the increases have stopped on the sleeves and are only worked on the front and back. *Work the front/back chart and then, when you have repeated the section in red and reached the next marker, work the sleeve chart.* When you have repeated the section in red and reach the next marker, repeat the section in stars once more. You should have worked a full round without increasing on the sleeves.

Size 4-5 and 6 raglan

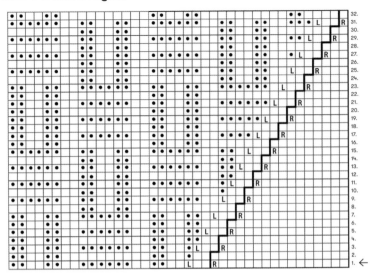

Size 4-5 sleeve

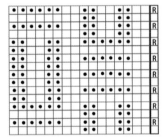

Size 4-5 front/back

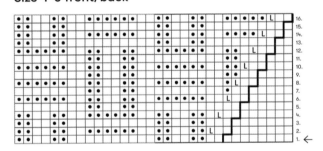

Size 6 sleeve

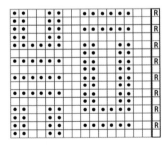

Size 6 front/back

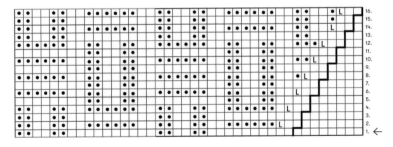

Upstream sweater charts

Size 7 raglan

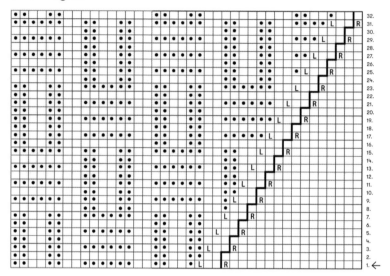

Size 7 sleeve

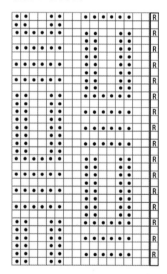

Size 7 front/back

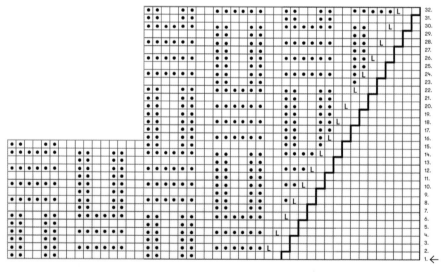

Size 8 raglan

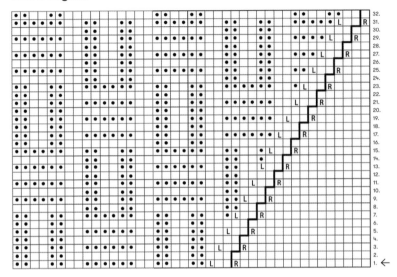

Size 8 sleeve

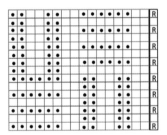

Size 8 front/back

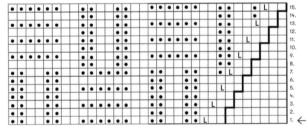

Wave vest charts

Size 1 repeat

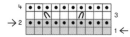

Size 1 left back

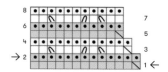

Size 1 right back

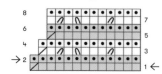

Size 1 left front

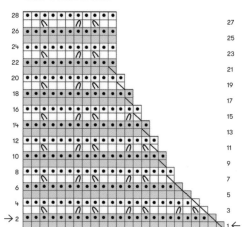

Size 1 right front

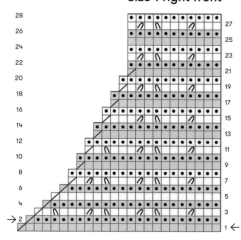

Size 2 left back

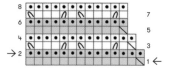

Size 2 right back

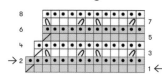

Size 2 left front

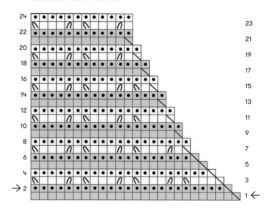

Size 2 right front

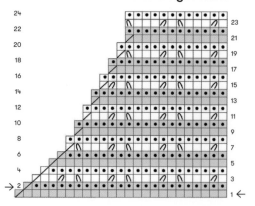

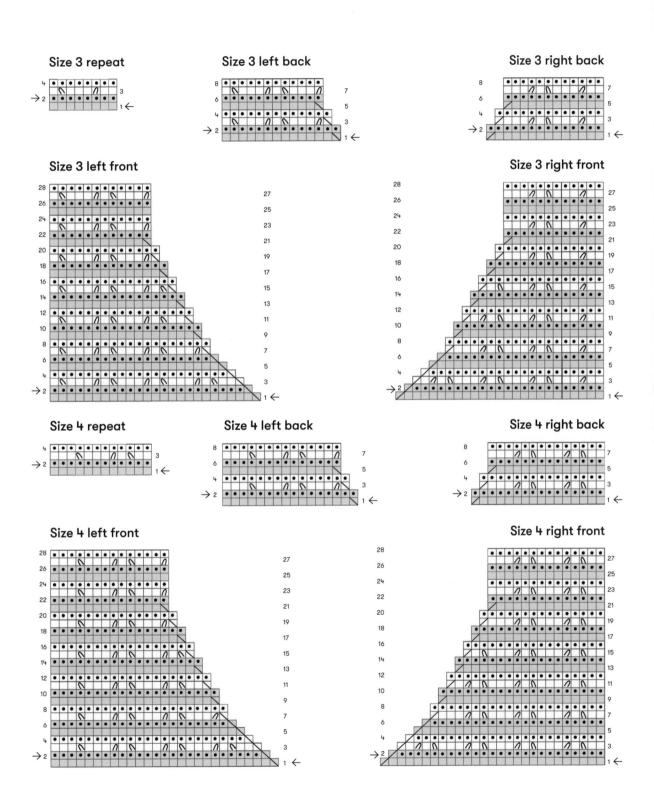

Size 3 repeat

Size 3 left back

Size 3 right back

Size 3 left front

Size 3 right front

Size 4 repeat

Size 4 left back

Size 4 right back

Size 4 left front

Size 4 right front

Wave vest charts

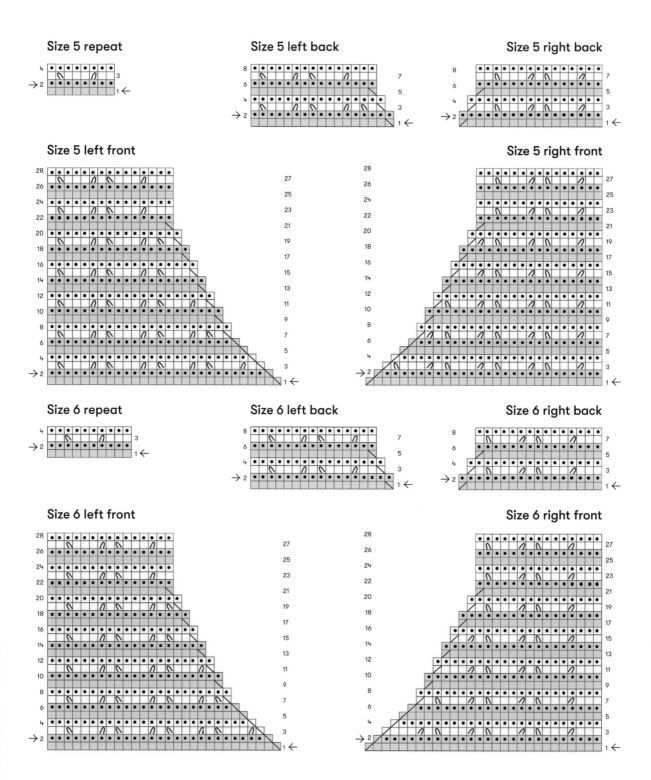

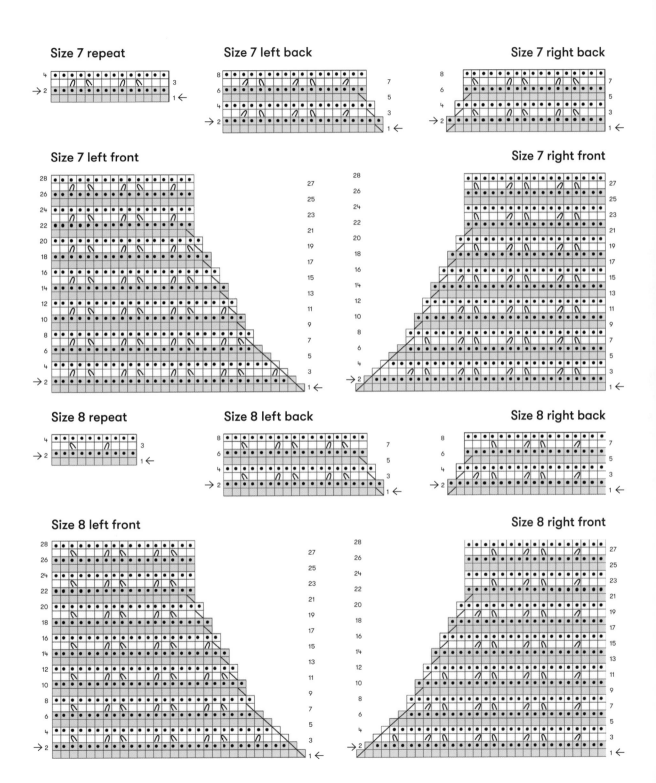

Size 7 repeat

Size 7 left back

Size 7 right back

Size 7 left front

Size 7 right front

Size 8 repeat

Size 8 left back

Size 8 right back

Size 8 left front

Size 8 right front

Ziggy sweater charts

Size 1 left front

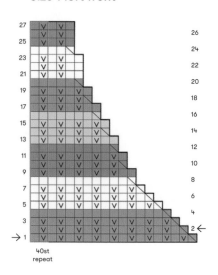

40st
repeat

Size 1 right front

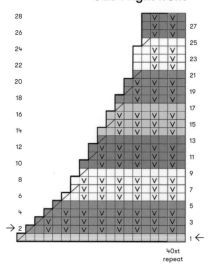

40st
repeat

Size 2 and 3 left front

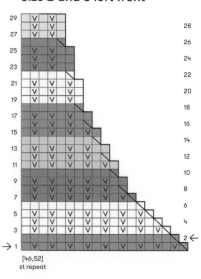

[46,52]
st repeat

Size 2 and 3 right front

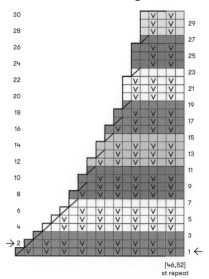

[46,52]
st repeat

Size 4 left front

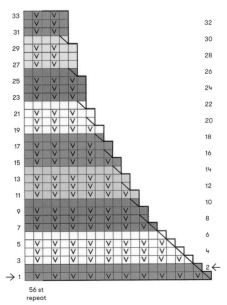

56 st
repeat

Size 4 right front

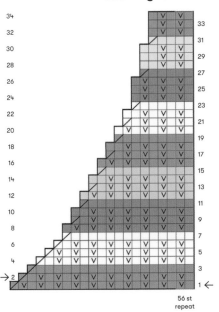

56 st
repeat

Size 5 left front

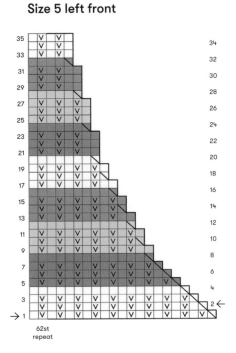

62st
repeat

Size 5 right front

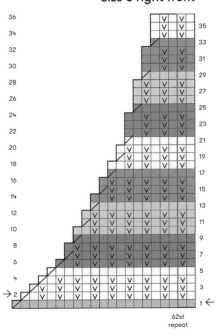

62st
repeat

Ziggy sweater charts

Size 6 left front

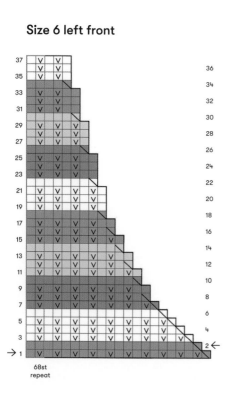

68st
repeat

Size 6 right front

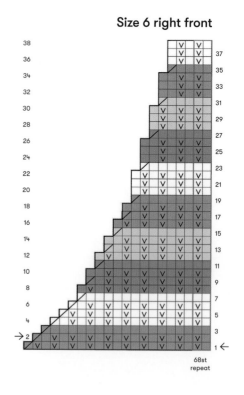

68st
repeat

Size 7 left front

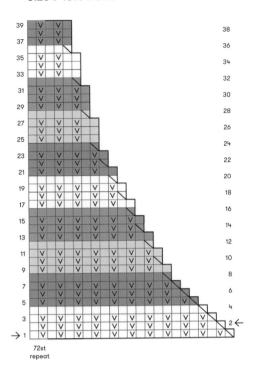

72st repeat

Size 7 right front

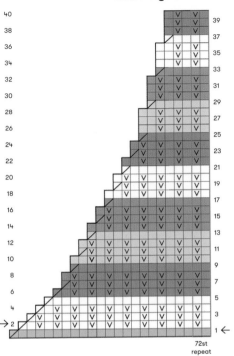

72st repeat

Size 8 left front

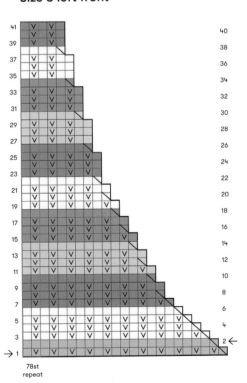

78st repeat

Size 8 right front

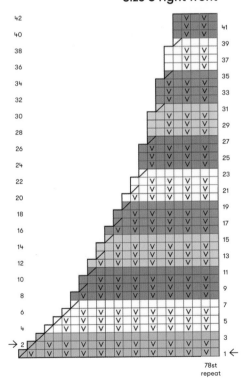

78st repeat

Off grid charts

Color key

B   C

Size 1 and 2 strap 1

Size 1 strap 2

Size 3 and 4 strap 1

Size 3 and 4 strap 2

Size 5 strap 1

Size 5 strap 2

Size 6 and 7 strap 1

WS → 5
4 ← RS
3 ← RS
WS → 2
WS → 1

Size 6 and 7 strap 2

WS → 5
4 ← RS
3 ← RS
WS → 2
WS → 1

Size 7 strap 3

WS → 5
4 ← RS
3 ← RS
WS → 2
WS → 1

Size 7 strap 4

WS → 5
4 ← RS
3 ← RS
WS → 2
WS → 1

Size 8 strap 1

WS → 5
4 ← RS
3 ← RS
WS → 2
WS → 1

Size 8 strap 2

WS → 5
4 ← RS
3 ← RS
WS → 2
WS → 1

Size 8 strap 3

WS → 5
4 ← RS
3 ← RS
WS → 2
WS → 1

Size 8 strap 4

WS → 5
4 ← RS
3 ← RS
WS → 2
WS → 1

Finishing and care

We often recommend blocking your knits to even out the stitches and assist in achieving the correct measurements. If you are happy with the way your piece has turned out, it's not mandatory, but blocking can sometimes significantly enhance the fit.

In certain circumstances, steam blocking can be more effective—for example, when making a large piece such as the Mix up blanket, you can steam block along the way. To do this, pin out the piece to the desired measurements, then hover the iron or steamer a few inches away while applying steam. Alternatively, you can use a damp towel or cloth to cover the piece and apply direct steam. Ensure you allow the piece to fully dry.

Refer to the blocking instructions for a specific yarn you are using or follow these guidelines:

1. Wash by hand in cool water, separately from other items. You can do this by running a bath or using a sink. Add wool wash or detergent. Place in the water and soak for around 10–15 minutes.

2. Lift out of the water and, supporting the weight evenly, gently squeeze out any excess water.

3. Place between two dry towels and roll the towels up to remove any moisture.

4. Pin out the piece to the pattern measurements on blocking mats or a towel. Make sure you do not stretch any ribs out we recommend leaving them as they are.

5. Leave until completely dry.

To give your knits a long and healthy life, here are a few simple steps you can take:

- There's no need to wash your knits regularly. Instead, try airing them out to ventilate. When washing is necessary, follow the steps outlined above.
- Always store your knits folded to avoid stretching; never hang them as the weight can stretch the garment out of shape. If possible, fold away somewhere contained to protect against pesky moths.
- Pilling can occur naturally with friction. Use a pilling comb or fabric shaver to easily remove.
- If a hole appears, patching and darning techniques are a great way to cover it. Textile artists are finding beautiful methods to mend—see books in our resources (page 172).

Your knits

Here's some inspiration from our amazing community, showcasing how they have made some of the designs in this book. Share and explore more knits through the pattern name hashtags on social media.

@ylvadesign_

@leahfoseid

@tarasvs

@annadasnes

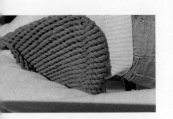

@bibicepiets

@the.social.fabric

@snmah

@cojicoji_co

@from.kathi

@shaandoran

@mick.knit

Jelena Wong

Resources

Check out our TikTok (@rows_knitwear) for regular stitch tutorials and our YouTube channel (@rows_knitwear) to help you with the patterns in this book.

Helpful tutorials on our channels:
Repurposing fabric into yarn
Folded cast off (bind off)
Twisted woven stitch, row 1
Sk3, p3 over, p3
Crossing yarns for the Static mittens
Adding a two-color I-cord to your Static mittens
Double linen stitch
Scrap thrumming
Looped stripe stitch

We use @woolandthegang, @verypinkknits or @purlsoho YouTube channels to remind ourselves of more general techniques such as:
Cable and long tail cast on
Stocking stitch (stockinette stitch)
Garter stitch
1 x 1 and 2 x 2 rib stitch
Slip stitches
Increases
Decreases
Casting off (binding off)
Picking up stitches
German short rows
Invisible seaming techniques
Whip stitch
Weaving in loose ends
Magic loop

A few wonderful yarn shops:
Wild and Woolly, London
Tangled yarn, Cheshire
Loop, London
Knit with Attitude, London
Breien en Zo, Haarlem
Sticks and Cups, Utrecht
Wol Verhalen, Tynaarlo
Cross and Woods, Den Haag
Hooks and Yarn, Amsterdam
Stephen and Penelope, Amsterdam
Yuzawaya, Tokyo
Masuzakiya, Osaka

Books and magazines:
The Harmony Guide to Knitting Stitches series
1000 Japanese Knitting and Crochet Stitches by Nihon Vogue
Embroidery on Knitting by Britt-Marie Christoffersson
On Mending: Stories of Damage and Repair by Celia Pym
Clothing Correspondence: Mending Stories and Darning Guide by Bronwen Jones
The Art of Repair: Mindful Mending by Molly Martin
Make Do and Mend (facsimile) by the Ministry of Information
A Dictionary of Color Combinations by Sanzo Wada
Press and Fold magazine (notes on making and doing fashion)
Tools magazine

Acknowledgements

THANK YOU

To Kyle Books and everyone who worked so hard on this book, especially Samhita, thank you for making this all happen.

A huge thank you to Candy, for understanding ROWS to the core, for always elevating my work with your beautiful design direction, and for your supportive friendship throughout.

To my amazing Tech Editors for all the invaluable pattern advice.

To Brooke for capturing these incredible images and for being an absolute dream to work with. To Lydia, Iris, and Sana for bringing our vision to life. To Amanda from Slocw Studio for lending some of your beautiful pieces for the shoot and to Saskia for the last-minute wardrobe raid!

To Wool and the Gang, Quince & Co, and Kremke Soul Wool for kindly sponsoring me with some beautiful yarns.

A special thanks to my family. Mum, Tom, and Poppy, I am so grateful for your endless support, and to my dad, who I wish could have seen this book. Elliott, I am extremely thankful for all your help and for your encouragement, patience, and support throughout this process. And to my wonderful friends, thank you for inspiring me and for being my cheerleaders on this journey.

Finally, thank you to the ROWS community for your ongoing support and inspiration. This would not have been possible without you!

Index

An Hachette UK Company
www.hachette.co.uk

First published in Great Britain in 2024 by Kyle Books,
an imprint of Octopus Publishing Group Limited
Carmelite House
50 Victoria Embankment
London EC4Y 0DZ

www.octopusbooks.co.uk
www.octopusbooksusa.com

ISBN 978-1-80419-257-3

Distributed in the US by
Hachette Book Group
1290 Avenue of the Americas
4th and 5th Floors
New York, NY 10104

Distributed in Canada by
Canadian Manda Group
664 Annette St.
Toronto, Ontario, Canada M6S 2C8

Printed and bound in China.
10 9 8 7 6 5 4 3 2 1

Publisher:
Joanna Copestick

Junior Commissioning Editor:
Samhita Foria

Art Director:
Nicky Collings

Design:
Candy Hutton

Photography:
Brooke Harwood

Illustrations:
Evie Dunne

Production:
Caroline Alberti